Thomas Cook

HOTSPOTS
CUBA

C000054397

Written by Jane Egginton and Iain MacIntyre
Front cover photography courtesy of Thomas Cook Tour Operations Ltd

Original design concept by Studio 183 Limited
Series design by the Bridgewater Book Company
Cover design/artwork by Lee Biggadike, Studio 183 Limited

Produced by the Bridgewater Book Company
The Old Candlemakers, West Street, Lewes, East Sussex BN7 2NZ, United Kingdom
www.bridgewaterbooks.co.uk
Project Editor: Emily Casey Bailey
Project Designer: Lisa McCormick

Published by Thomas Cook Publishing
A division of Thomas Cook Tour Operations Limited
PO Box 227, Units 15-16, Coningsby Road, Peterborough PE3 8SB, United Kingdom
email: books@thomascook.com
www.thomascookpublishing.com
+ 44 (0) 1733 416477

ISBN 13: 978-1-84157-565-0
ISBN 10: 1-84157-565-8

First edition © 2006 Thomas Cook Publishing
Text © 2006 Thomas Cook Publishing
Maps © 2006 Thomas Cook Publishing
Head of Thomas Cook Publishing: Chris Young
Project Editor: Diane Ashmore
Production/DTP Editor: Steven Collins

Printed and bound in Spain by Graficas Cems, Navarra, Spain

CONTENTS

SYMBOLS KEY

The following is a key to the symbols used throughout this book:

i information office	train station	restaurant
bus stop	airport	café
post office	tip	fine dining
church	shopping	

🕿 telephone   📠 fax   ✉ email   🌐 website address

ⓐ address   🕐 opening times   ❶ important

€ budget price   €€ mid-range price   €€€ most expensive

★ specialist interest   ★★ see if passing   ★★★ top attraction

---

Florida Keys
USA

GULF OF MEXICO

HAVANA
VARADERO
MARIEL
MANTANZAS
CARDENAS
GÜINES
GÜIRA DE
MÉLENA
SURGIDERO
DE BATABANÓ
JOVELLANOS
COLÓN
MINAS DE
MATAHAMBRE
PINAR DEL RIO
AGUADA DE
PASAJEROS
SANTA CLARA
ARROYOS
DE MANTUA
GUANE
Golfo de
Batabanó
CIENFUEGOS
LA FE
SP
T

Yucatan Channel

**ISLA
DE LA
JUVENTUD**
Bay of Pigs

**CAYO
LARGO**

CARIBBEAN SEA

CANADA

UNITED STATES
OF AMERICA
Atlantic
Ocean

Gulf of
Mexico
HAVANA
CUBA

MEXICO

Pacific
Ocean
Caribbean
Sea

Cayman Islands
(UK)

N

| 0 | | 100 km |
| 0 | | 60 miles |

Getting to know Cuba

Cuba is the largest of the Caribbean islands, 150 km (93 miles) south of Florida's Key West, but it gets just a fraction of the tourists of nearby Jamaica. Only 35 km (22 miles) at its narrowest point, its slender shape and lush vegetation led Nicolás Guillén, the Cuban national poet, to describe his homeland as 'a long green lizard'.

Cuba today is inextricably linked with its history. The country is truly unique and really getting to know it takes time. Still charismatic, though decidedly getting on in years, Fidel Castro has been in power since the Revolution in 1959, and is the world's longest serving head of state. He also holds the record for the longest speech (made to the UN and lasting over four hours), and continues to address his people through television broadcasts that regularly last several hours.

Many Cubans see Castro as a teenager would a strict but loving father. On the one hand, he has delivered free health care and education systems that would put most 'developed' countries to shame. On the other, he imposes tight controls on everyday life, limiting what people can buy, do and even say. One aspect of this is that crime is severely punished and tourist areas heavily policed, so that beaches and streets are relatively free of hassle and crime.

LIFESTYLE

The first thing to remember when you land in Cuba is that you have just entered one of the world's last bastions of centrally controlled socialism. Since the revolution in 1959, its government has delivered free and universal housing, health and education to the people of this island, but freedom of speech is restricted, the only newspapers are government-run. Very few Cubans have the Internet in their home or even a computer. Open criticism of the government is not tolerated, and freedom of movement is restricted.

However, although the strength of the people is tested regularly by '*la lucha*' ('the daily struggle'), Cubans positively assert '*Todo se resuelve*'

Havana's Ministry of the Interior building sports Che Guevara's mural and slogan

('everything will sort itself out'). Despite all the challenges they have to face, Cubans are some of the most generous, gracious and funny people you are likely to meet. They are nothing if not determined, and necessity being the mother of invention, the country is gradually bouncing back, and is even beginning to show signs of thriving. Cuba is proud that after hundreds of years of foreign intervention (Spanish, English, American, Soviet) it is now standing on its own two feet.

FORMER PLAYGROUND

Cuba is not a newcomer to tourism. From the 1920s the country was a notorious playground for American millionaires, gangsters and artists.

Initially these pleasure-seekers came to escape Prohibition, and live it up on the beach, with Havana in particular gaining a reputation as a hedonistic mecca of dancing girls, gambling and drinking.

All that came to a halt with the Revolution in 1959, and Cuba, forbidden to trade with the US, turned to Moscow as a trading partner – a relationship that lasted until the collapse of the Soviet Union in the early 1990s. With his biggest ally in crisis, and facing losses of US\$5 billion in annual revenue, Castro has more recently turned his attention to tourism as a way of filling the empty state coffers.

REFRESHINGLY DIFFERENT

The ever-present economic crisis and the departure of nearly a quarter of the population has divided many families. However, one of the blessings for the visitor is that the country is free of the commercialism that plagues so many other countries and there is a welcome absence of faceless chain restaurants and shops. Top international beach resorts have been built to cater for visitors and the rest of the country is relatively unspoilt by tourism – many fine historic centres remain. This makes Cuba a great place to combine a beach holiday with a dip into local culture.

It is best not to bring up questions about Castro or politics in public places. Many Cubans are happy to talk if there is no chance of being overheard, but even so, try to be tactful and listen, rather than offer your own opinion on such complex matters.

TOURISM, CUBAN-STYLE

The country's tourism industry is managed almost entirely by government-run agencies, which certainly lends Cuba a different flavour to most tourist destinations. The City Historian manages the regeneration of Old Havana under the auspices of UNESCO (which declared the city a World Heritage Site in 1982). This means that fine old buildings are being carefully restored and converted into museums, boutique hotels and plush restaurants. The streets are kept spotless, and violent crime is almost unheard of. There is, however, some way to go. Service standards fall far below those to be found in more Westernised countries; state-run restaurant food is, with some exceptions, mediocre, and service can be very slow.

But a new, outward-looking attitude, along with the island's idyllic beaches, clear blue waters, year-round sun and friendly people, means that the future looks bright for Cuba.

CUBAN TRANSPORT

Even if they could afford it, most Cubans are not allowed to buy a car. Some have inherited old American cars from their grandfathers, and the odd overseas worker who earned a bit of hard currency has been allowed to spend it on a new car, but such cases are few and far between. Many old cars are used as *collectivos* – group taxis which head into the city in the morning and out in the evening.

All public transport is overcrowded and unreliable. *Camellos*, little more than converted, articulated lorries, are packed to bursting everyday with uncomplaining city dwellers trying to get to work – and these are the lucky ones. Trains run between some of the major cities, but for Cubans, tickets are expensive and difficult to come by. A large section of the population is forced to hitchhike, whether its getting home to the suburbs after a hard day's work in Havana, or taking their child on a 40 km (25 mile) hike from the sugar plantation to the nearest hospital. Cubans spend a great deal of their lives just trying to get from A to B. For holiday-makers here, things are a lot easier, but any journey can still prove a challenge (see page 114).

The best of Cuba

ISLAND LIFE

Cuba is a big country. Apart from the main island, there are another 4,000 islands and coral cays, most of which are uninhabited. These range in size from a tiny trio near Guardalavaca to the much larger tourist resorts of **Cayo Largo** and **Cayo Coco** (see pages 50 and 54); even **Varadero** (see page 39) is practically an island. Together they feature 300 beaches, from enormous, blinding-white stretches to secluded, pretty coves surrounded by lush vegetation. The Atlantic Ocean lies to the north of Cuba, while the Caribbean laps the southern shore, forming a backdrop to all kinds of water sports. The country boasts one of the largest coral reefs in the world and the diving here is world-class.

CUBAN PEOPLE

A definite highlight of any trip to Cuba is its people, who are by nature warm, smiling and thoughtful, whether giggling schoolgirls or swaggering cowboys. While the better hotels and upmarket resorts are reserved only for international tourists, try to make contact with the locals (other than those who approach you on the street) whenever you can, as you will surely be rewarded. These people will do almost anything for you, and despite their predicament, rarely ask for anything in return.

TO BARE OR NOT TO BARE

Topless sunbathing on beaches is likely to be deeply offensive to locals, although it may be possible around the pool in some hotels and is becoming more common in resorts such as Varadero and Cayo Coco. So if you dare to bare, choose your location carefully.

LIVING HISTORY

The country's rich cultural past is not found in gloomy museums or on dusty archaeological sites, but in its central squares that buzz with activity, in its lived-in buildings and giant 1950s American cars, and out in the lush countryside. Many of the crumbling buildings in **Old Havana** (see page 19) are architectural gems and there are several charming colonial towns, of which **Trinidad** (see page 75) is perhaps the best example. Nearby, sugar and coffee plantations in the **Valle de los Ingenios** (see page 76) are important both historically and economically, and offer scenic delights. All three of these locations have attained UNESCO world recognition and are popular excursions. Although the Revolution took place nearly 50 years ago, it is still very much in the hearts and minds of the people and it is easy to take a tour through 'Revolutionary Cuba' (see pages 80–84).

UNSPOILT NATURE

From well-visited **Viñales** (see page 73) in the west to remote **Baconoa** (see page 79) in the east, Cuba's landscape has dramatic mountains, tropical vegetation cut through by clear rivers, as well as living coral reefs, exotic plants and brightly coloured flowers. Take to the hills on foot or horseback or join a tour that will allow you to really enjoy the island's nature. Everything is within easy reach of the main resorts, whether you are a bird-spotter or an adventure tourist.

◀ *Most visitors are welcomed with smiles from the locals*

MUSIC

Cuban music is known throughout the world and sings out from every street corner. The beat of the African drum, a centuries-old heirloom from the slave trade, is seamlessly mixed with the more melodic Spanish guitar, reflecting the country's rich and diverse history. More contemporary forms have been influenced by Europe and the US, and Cuba continues to contribute to the world music arena. Young and old dance and sing at every opportunity and restaurants and historic **cabarets** (see pages 37–38 for Havana's cabaret venues) are perfect showcases for the country's talent.

CIGARS & RUM

Fat, aroma-filled cigars and sweet, strong rum are very much part of the country's flavour, and sold for such a price that you can afford to take a bit of Cuba home with you (see page 93). President Kennedy imported a stash of his favourite Upman cigars before declaring the blockade; in the old days Castro was rarely seen without a Cohiba in his mouth, while Che Guevara preferred Montecristos.

A tour of a **cigar factory** (see page 23), where workers roll out a staggering 65 million cigars a year, and of a rum distillery can offer a fascinating insight into everyday life, as well as allowing you to learn about production and inspect goods at first hand.

Havana Club is the most famous Cuban rum since the Bacardi family took their brand to Puerto Rico after the Revolution. The three- and five-year-old bottles are best used in cocktails (see page 90); superior seven-year-old rum is drunk neat or with ice as you would a fine whisky.

Havana
faded beauty

With its clean, cobbled streets, attractive, leafy squares and little evidence of street hustlers, Havana, or *La Habana*, is without doubt one of Latin America's most pleasant and enjoyable cities. Most buildings have seen better days, but they retain an air of faded grandeur, which adds to the city's charms. In 1982, Havana was declared a UNESCO World Heritage Site, and this kick-started a programme of restoration with architectural and historic treasures being brought back to life.

The biggest city in the Caribbean, Havana is a city of many parts, each of which has its own identity. **Habana Vieja (Old Havana)**, deep in the harbour mouth, was established in the 16th century and is the historic heart of the capital. **Habana Centro (Central Havana)**, which took form in the 1800s as a residential and recreational area outside the old city walls, has its share of fine old buildings and is also where the city's residents and tourists come to eat, drink and dance to the rhythm of Cuba's famous music.

Further east is **Vedado**, which was designed on a regular grid in 1859 but really took shape in the first half of the 20th century. It is a mixture of colonial mansions, parks and plazas, interspersed with modern high-rise offices, hotels and government buildings. Across the river are **Miramar** and **Playa**, leafy suburbs that before the Revolution were popular with Havana's elite. Today these areas are home to five-star hotels and foreign embassies.

Then there is the **Malecón**; this broad avenue following the sweep of the shore was conceived as a Mediterranean-style pedestrian promenade but it has become the main traffic thoroughfare connecting all of these areas together. Nonetheless, Cubans love to hang out on the sea wall, fishing, chatting, flirting and people watching. The Malecón's sea wall is also Havana's first line of defence against the raging storms that sweep in from the Caribbean. Many of the buildings along its length bear testament to the damage caused by recent hurricanes.

N

FORTALEZA DE LOS TRES REYES DEL MORO (EL MORRO CASTLE)

0   150   300 m
0   300 yds

1 MUSEO DE LA MÚSICA (NATIONAL MUSIC MUSEUM)

2 THEATRE

3 PALACIO DE LOS CAPITANES GENERALES/MUSEO DE LA CIUDAD

4 CÉSPEDES STATUE

5 MUSEO NACIONAL DE HISTORIA NATURAL

6 EL TEMPLETE

7 CASA DE LOS ARABES

8 HABANA 1791

9 MUSEO DE LA REVOLUCIÓN

10 GRANMA MEMORIAL

11 HOTEL SEVILLA

12 REAL FÁBRICA DE TABACOS PARTAGÁS

CASTILLO DE SAN SALVADOR DE LA PUNTA

STUDENT MONUMENT

MÁXIMO GÓMEZ

Canal de Entrada

CASTILLO DE SAN CARLOS DE LA CABAÑA

PLAYAS DEL ESTE →

MALECÓN

SAN LÁZARO

GENIOS

AV CARLOS M. CÉSPEDES

CUBA TACÓN

OLD WALL RUINS

PASEO DE MARTÍ (PRADO)

CONSULADO

CUARTELES

CHACÓN

TEJADILLO

EMPEDRADO

PROGRESO

AV DE LAS MISIONES

PALACIO DE BELLAS ARTES (NATIONAL MUSEUM)

PARQUE CÉSPEDES

CATEDRAL DE SAN CRISTOBEL

PLAZA DE ARMAS

CASTILLO DE LA REAL FUERZA

NEPTUNO

AV BÉLGICA

OBISPO

OBRAPIA

LAMPARILLA

AMARGURA

BASIL

COMPOSTELA

VILLEGAS

AGUIAR

SAN IGNACIO

COIN MUSEUM

AGRAMONTE

EL CAPITOLIO

OLD WALL RUINS

HABANA VIEJA (OLD HAVANA)

MURALLA

PLAZA VIEJA

MERCADERES

INQUISIDOR

OFICIOS

MUSEO DEL RON

DRAGONES

MARTI THEATRE

FUÉNTE DE LA INDIA

AV. SIMÓN BOLIVAR

MÁXIMO GOMEZ

CORRALES

APODACA

GLORIA

ECONOMIA

AGRAMONTE

EGIDO

SOL

LUZ

ACOSTA

CUBA

DAMAS

MERCED

LEONOR PÉREZ

SAN ISIDRO

DESAMPARADOS

SAN PEDRO

Ensenada de Atarés

THINGS TO SEE & DO (OLD HAVANA)
Plaza de Armas ★ ★ ★
For a bird's eye view of the area, take the lift to the rooftop bar in the
Museo Nacional de Historia Natural in Plaza de Armas (🕓 Open daily
July–Aug; Thurs–Sat Sept–June). Surrounded by historic buildings, this
colonial square is also home to a great second-hand book store, and
famous Cuban orchestras hold free concerts here every Friday evening.

Museo del Ron (Rum Museum) ★ ★ ★
Very worthwhile, with a bilingual guided tour that reveals rum-making
antiquities as well as the brewing process. There are also occasional
music events in the beautiful courtyard at 19.00. ❸ Fundación Havana
Club, San Pedro 262 e/ Sol (see page 113 for explanation of Cuban
addresses) ❶ (7) 8615 051 🕓 Mon–Fri 09.00–17.00, Sat and Sun 10.00–16.00

Palacio de los Capitanes Generales/Museo de la Ciudad ★ ★ ★
This palace, a baroque masterpiece, was completed in 1792 and was
commissioned by the Spanish Governor of the day as a strident symbol
of colonial power. From here, the Governor, known as the Captain
General, controlled the whole of Cuba on behalf of the Spanish Crown. In
1899, with the wars of independence all but won, the US intervened and
put the island under military occupation for three years, during which
time the American Governor lived in the Palacio. Afterwards, it was home
to repressive dictators installed by the Americans to protect US
interests. The building houses the **Museo de la Cuidad (City Museum)**,
where fine paintings and sculptures are on view in the opulent salons
that surround a peaceful leafy courtyard. ❸ Plaza de Armas e/ Obispo
❶ (7) 8615 779 🕓 Open 09.00–18.00 to the general public

El Templete ★ ★
On the corner of Plaza de Armas opposite the Palacio is a small building
shaded by a large ceiba tree. According to city legend, it was on this spot

◀ *A horse and cart ambles along Havana's colourful old streets*

under the leaves of a ceiba that Havana was founded in 1599. The tree is a focal point when Havana celebrates its foundation in November. Inside El Templete are paintings depicting the history of the city. ❷ Plaza de Armas e/ O'Reilly ❶ (7) 8612 876 ❸ Open 09.30–18.00

Catedral de San Cristóbal ★★

Named after the locals' belief that the cathedral once housed the remains of Christopher Colombus, this 18th-century church dominates the Plaza de la Catedral. The imposing Baroque exterior gives way to a standard Latin cross interior. After the fall of Communism, Castro softened his stance on religion and Pope John Paul II celebrated Mass in the cathedral in 1998. Since then, the government has allowed Christmas Day to once again be celebrated. ❷ Calle Emperado 156 ❶ (7) 8617 1771 ❸ Open Mon–Fri 10.30–15.30, Sat 10.30–14.30, Sun 09.00–12.30; morning Mass, Sun 10.30; evening Mass Tues, Thurs and Fri 20.30

Castillo de la Real Fuerza ★★

Just north of the Plaza de Armas is this moated fortress. Finished in 1577, it was intended as a bulwark against marauding French and English pirates. Havana was a weigh station for the gold looted from South America, but Spanish naval planners were occasionally inept. It soon transpired that the fort had been constructed in the wrong place and provided little defence, which is probably why it is still standing. ❷ Calle Tacón e/ Obispo ❶ (7) 8616 130 ❸ Open 09.00–18.30

Forteleza de los Tres Reyes de Moro (el Morro Castle) ★★★

After the disaster of Real Fuerza, the Spanish commissioned an Italian to design this fortress overlooking Old Havana from a headland on the Eastern side of the harbour. Work began in 1589, although the current lighthouse dates from the mid-19th century. ❷ Carretera de la Cabaña ❶ (7) 8620 617 ❸ Open 10.00–22.00

---

❶ *Castillo de la Real Fuerza overlooks Old Havana*

Enlarged map – page 17

Canal de Entrada

Habana Vieja
(Old Havana)

COIN MUSEUM

Ensenada de Atarés

DESAMPARADO SAN PEDRO

AV CARLOS M. CESPEDES

EGIDO

MÁXIMO GÓMEZ

PASEO DE MARTI (PRADO)

EL CAPITOLIO

MÁXIMO GÓMEZ

CASTILLO DE ATARÉS

Luyanó

MALECON

19

3

Habana Centro
(Central Havana)

AVENIDA SIMON BOLIVAR

PADRE VARELA

Caleta de San Lázaro

CALZADA DE INFANTA

VIA BLANCA

Santos Suárez

VIA BLANCA

AVENIDA SALVADOR ALLENDE

HOTEL NACIONAL

CALZADA DE INFANTA

16

9

ARTS & CRAFTS MARKET

5

1

3

UNIVERSIDAD DE LA HABANA
(UNIVERSITY OF HAVANA)

CALZADA DE AYESTARAN

2

12

4

LA RAMPA

AVENIDA RANCHO BOYEROS

CASTILLO DE PRINCIPE

AVENIDA DA CARLOS M. DE CESPEDES

CALZADA DE ZAPATA

6

7

8

PALACIO DE LA REVOLUCIÓN

AVENIDA DE LA INDEPENDENCIA

AVENIDA DE LOS PRESIDENTES

Vedado

ALZADA

LINEA

PASEO

LA RAMPA

MARIANAO

15

Nuevo Vedado

NATIONAL ZOO

NECROPOLIS CRISTOBEL COLON
(CRISTOBAL COLÓN CEMETERY)

BOTANICA GARDEN

MALECON

1 USS MAINE MONUMENT	**5** HABANA LIBR
2 TEATRO NACIONAL DE GUIÑOL	**6** PLAZA DE LA REVOLUCION
3 PABELLON CUBA	**7** JOSÉ MARTI MONUMENT
4 COPPELIA PARK	**8** NATIONAL THEATRE

0   300 m
0   300 yds

THINGS TO SEE & DO (CENTRAL HAVANA)
El Capitolio ★ ★ ★
Visit this building in the heart of Havana, and you may experience a
sense of deja vu. Modelled after America's famous seat of government
in Washington, Cuba's El Capitolio was built in the 1920s, and housed
the Cuban government until the Revolution. Now home to the Cuban
Academy of Sciences, all road distances in Cuba are measured from
here. The entrance hall is dominated by the Statue of the Republic, a 17 m
(56 foot) tall, gold-covered statue of Jupiter that was shipped from Rome.

You can walk around the Chamber of Deputies, frozen in time with
its original furniture, and visit the impressive library that is modelled on
the Vatican's own. The area around El Capitolio is alive with bars, street
artists and contraband cigar sellers. Sit on the steps of el Capitolio and
have your picture taken with an antique camera, then watch the print
be developed before your eyes. ❷ Paseo de Marti (Prado) e/ San José
❶ (7) 8603 411 ❸ Open 08.30–19.00

Real Fábrica de Tabacos Partagás ★ ★ ★
This one of the oldest cigar factories in Havana. You can take a tour with
an English-speaking guide and see the workers, mostly women, at their
fascinating craft. Even if you don't pay for the tour, the cigar shop just
inside the entrance is worth a look. On sale are a selection of Cuba's
finest cigars, and some exquisite cigar boxes and humidors. ❷ Calle
Industria 524, on the corner of Parque Central behind El Capitolio
❶ (7) 8624 604 ❸ Open Mon–Sat 09.30–11.00 and 2.30–15.00

Paseo de Marti (Prado) ★ ★ ★
This pleasant, tree-lined avenue runs from El Capitolio all the way to the
Malecón. Designed in 1772 as a place for Havana's elite to promenade and
ride in their carriages, it is still popular with the city's residents. You might
see the odd street musician or mime artist, but on the whole it is just an
attractive place where Cubans relax during lunchtime and stroll in the
evening. Historic buildings abound, such as **Hotel Sevilla**, with its Moorish
architecture, on the corner of Calle Trocadero.

Palacio de Bellas Artes (National Museum) ★★★

Spacious and contemporary, this museum is home to some of the
finest art in the Americas, such as *La Habana en Rojo* (1962) by René
Portocarrero. ⓐ San Rafael e/ Zulueta ⓣ (7) 8621 643 ⓛ Open Tues–Sat
10.00–18.00, Sun 10.00–14.00 ⓘ Admission charge

Museo de la Revolución ★★★

It is fitting that the Museum of the Revolution was set up in the former
presidential palace of the dictator Batista. The exhibits tell the story
of the Revolution from the day that a band of just 80 guerillas landed
on the shores of Eastern Cuba in a tiny launch boat named *Granma*
(on display opposite the museum). ⓐ Calle Refugio 1 e/ Missiones
ⓣ (7) 8624 091 ⓛ Open 10.00–1700

 If you visit a museum in the afternoon but run out of time, ask to
have your ticket signed so that you can return the next day to see
more of the exhibits.

THINGS TO SEE & DO (VEDADO)
Vedado Walking Tour ★★★

A good place to start a walking tour of Havana is the **USS *Maine*
Monument**, which is on the Malecón at the bottom of Calle 17. In 1898,
when the Spanish and Americans where arguing over who should
control Cuba, the US battleship USS *Maine* mysteriously exploded while
at anchor close to Havana. Most of the senior officers were ashore at
the time, but 266 sailors met their death. The Americans blamed the
Spanish, the Spanish said it was an accident, and in later years, some
claimed the US had blown up their own ship as an excuse to start a
war they knew they could win. The victorious Americans raised this
monument to their dead, but the American Eagle that once topped
the twin pillars has been removed, and an inscription added, alluding
to the avarice of imperialism.

From the monument, you have a great view of the twin towers of
the **Hotel Nacional** (see page 27). Stroll round to Calle 'O', and walk up

🔺 *Máximo Gómez monument, Havana*

◖ *Royal Palms guard El Capitolio, Havana*

the grand, palm-lined entrance, where vintage taxis wait to ferry the well-to-do around the city,

From the Nacional, continue down Calle 'O', and turn right onto 'La Rampa' (Calle 23). This famous street is home to the **Pabellón Cuba**, a modernist concrete building where art exhibitions are held. Across the street is the **Vedado Arts & Crafts Market**. Alongside the Che Guevara t-shirts, there are stalls selling shoes and other essentials to ordinary Cubans. Just past the market is the huge **Habana Libre** hotel, once part of the Hilton chain. Conrad Hilton himself opened the hotel as a playground for America's rich, but the Revolution intervened shortly afterwards. The walls on the first floor are lined with photographs from the hotel's past, including one of Che Guevara taking part in a chess contest there.

From the Habana Libre, turn left and follow the road three blocks to where the **Universidad de La Habana** sits on the hill. Today, students on their lunch break relax on the steep steps that lead to the University, but in the days of the dictators, angry demonstrations where held here, and you can see the **Monument to Julio Antonia Mella**, a student leader murdered by agents of Machado (a US-backed Cuban leader) in 1929.

When you come across *jiniteros* (street hustlers) in Havana, they may say they are studying at the University, and then ask for money to feed their family. Whilst this is a common ruse, the university is a major seat of learning, where 30,000 students a year receive a higher education – a greater proportion then any other country in Latin America.

Hotel Nacional ★★

Opened in 1930, this opulent hotel has a colourful history. Gangsters, film stars, millionaires and presidents have all stayed here. It played its part in the *coup d'etat* that brought the dictator Batista to power (this is where officers loyal to his predecessor where captured) and in 1958, the New Year's Eve party was in full swing when news broke that Batista had fled the country, and Castro was heading for Havana. Wealthy, panic-stricken foreigners, mostly American, ran for their yachts and private planes, leaving behind opulent Cadillacs, Chevrolets and Plymouths, which fell into the hands of the people. Through the lobby is a fine, cloistered garden where you can enjoy a cocktail, or stroll down to the terrace for a spectacular view of the seafront.

Plaza de la Revolución ★ ★ ★

Batista built this great city square, but it had just been finished and named Plaza de la República when he was swept away by the tide of revolt in 1959. In the early sixties, Castro addressed crowds of up to a million people here as he attempted to counter US propaganda with his oratory. The centre-piece of the square is the José Marti Monument (see below), which faces the Ministry of the Interior and an imposing mural of Che Guevara featuring his slogan '*Hasta La Victoia Siempre*' ('Towards Victory Always'). The austere building behind the monument is home to the Central Committee of the Communist Party of Cuba, and it is here that Castro has his office.

José Marti Monument ★ ★ ★

When addressing crowds, Castro stands beneath this enormous statue of Cuba's national hero José Marti, poet, politician and independence fighter who died in battle against the Spanish in 1895. Towering over this is a star-shaped obelisk, 139 m (456 ft) high, where you can view some of Marti's work, and other exhibits about his life. Take the lift to the top for a great city view.

Necropólis Cristobel Colón ★ ★

Not as macabre as it sounds, a visit to the Necrópolis, as it

🔵 *José Marti watches over Havana*

⬥ The glorious, palm-lined entrance to the historic Hotel Nacional

⬥ *The controversial USS* Maine *Monument, Havana*

is known here, is a must for visitors. More than a million graves are spread out over an area of 30 city blocks, with amazing headstones, monuments and statues spread throughout. Home to Havana's dead, both rich and poor, this is also the place where a young Fidel Castro, at the funeral of a friend who had killed himself in an act of protest, jumped up and gave a rousing condemnation of the dictator Batista.

ⓐ Calle Zapata e/ Calle 12 ❶ (7) 8334 196 ❶ Open 08.00–17.00

EXCURSIONS
Hemingway's Mile ★★

For his Nobel Prize-winning book, *The Old Man of the Sea* (1952), Ernest Hemingway took inspiration from the village of **Cojímar**, and the fishermen who made it their home. Hemingway made his first visit to Cuba in 1928, and fell in love with it. In 1939, he bought his house, Finca Vigía, close to the city of Havana, where he lived sporadically until 1960. After 1962, when Hemingway gave his estate to the people of Cuba, it became the **Museo Hemingway** (ⓐ Calle Vigía e/ Steinhard ❶ Open Wed–Mon 09.00–16.00).

Here, everything is as the American author left it, and his spirit lives on. It still contains his library of 8,000 books, important artworks, an idiosyncratic cat cemetery and *Pilar* – the author's fishing boat. Hemingway was an avid deep-sea angler, spending much of his time on the coast hunting the sailfish that fill these waters. A fishing tournament he set up is still held every year in May. In 1960, when Castro was its winner, the competition became the stuff of legend.

When the world-famous writer died, the local, impoverished fishermen melted down their anchors and fishing gear and had a bust of Hemingway cast. It now stands in the tiny town square of Cojímar that bears his name.

The appealing restaurant and cocktail lounge, **La Terraza**, was a Hemingway favourite, and today is a popular spot to drink a toast to his memory while looking out over the bay. There are daily organized tours here, or you can hire a car.

Playas del Este ★★

Havana's Riviera, just a 20-minute drive from the city, is a 48 km (30 mile) stretch of pleasant sandy beach and clear water, popular with Cubans. Havana's nearest beach is **Playa Bacuranao**, but more scenic spots lie beyond. Tree-backed **Santa María del Mar** is probably the most visited by day trippers. **Guanabo** has a number of tourist facilities, but can get crowded at weekends. Divers flock to the **Bajo de las Lavanders**.

⬤ *Browsing in the second-hand book market in Plaza de Armas*

SHOPPING

 Many of the larger hotels, such as Hotel Nacional and Hostal Valencia (see Restaurant Paella page 36), as well as the cigar factory, **Real Fábrica de Tabacos Partagás** (see page 23), house a **Casa del Tobacco**, or tobacco shop. Although you will be offered cigars on the street for a fraction of the price of these outlets, they are likely to be fakes (see page 93).

A colourful **second-hand book market** in Plaza de Armas (see page 19) has some fascinating old titles. Most titles are in Spanish, but there are some English books and guides (🕑 Open Wed–Sat 10.00–19.00; daily in December).

Habana 1791 is housed in a beautiful, stained-glass building and sells perfumes, jewellery and glass and ceramic perfume bottles (➌ Calle de los Mercaderes 156 e/ Obrapia).

Valle de Viñales ★★★

Little more than a two-hour drive west of Havana is this fertile valley, best explored by walking or horse-riding tours. Nearby, the colonial town of **Pinar del Río**, named after the great swathes of pine trees that once stood here, has a couple of local museums, as well as a brandy distillery and cigar factory.

RESTAURANTS (see maps on pages 17 and 22)

Finding a good meal in Havana is not as difficult as it once was. There are still countless, state-run restaurants serving mediocre food at inflated prices, but some reasonably good establishments can be found. Then there are *paladares* – harder to find, these are small, privately owned places where the food is often cheaper and more varied, and usually accompanied by a healthy dose of conversation with real Cubans. If a street-hustler takes you to one of these restaurants, you will pay a commission on top of your meal, so it's better to seek them out yourself or ask people you trust.

Café del Oriente € ❶ (*see page 17*) You can enjoy set meals here in a spacious, sunny courtyard surrounded by tropical plants. ⓐ Oficios e/ Amargura ❶ (7) 860 6686 🕒 Open 10.00–22.00

Castillo de Farnes €€ ❷ (*see page 17*) Enjoy a great mojito in this local pavement bar near the touristy El Floridita restaurant. The intimate restaurant offers Spanish specialties, as well as lobster, steak, fish and a great value set menu. Don't miss the photograph of Che and Fidel, who was a regular, celebrating the victorious 1959 Revolution in the restaurant. ⓐ Calle Monserrate e/ Obrapía ❶ (7) 867 1030 🕒 Open noon–midnight

Chinatown € ❸ (*see page 22*) This tiny Chinese enclave is home to a few small and basic restaurants. ⓐ Calle Zanja e/ Rayo 🕒 Open noon–midnight

Dominica €€€ ❹ (*see page 17*) Just off Plaza de Armas, this Italian restaurant has decent pasta, great carpaccio and fine wine and seafood. Sit outside and enjoy the live bands. ⓐ Calle O'Reilly esq. a Mercaderes ❶ (7) 860 2918 🕒 Open noon–midnight

Jardin del Eden €€€ ❺ (*see page 17*) Part of the Hotel Raquel, all the usual dishes are on the menu, plus vegetarian options, curry and goulash, in a grand dining room with marbled floors, pillars and high ceilings. ⓐ Calle Amargura 103 e/ San Ignacio ❶ (7) 860 8280

Jardin del Oriente €€€ ❻ (*see page 17*) Popular and grand restaurant with live piano music. Frogs' legs, lobster medallions and Chateau Briande are all on the menu. ⓐ Oficios 112 e/ Amargura ❶ (7) 860 6686 🕒 Open noon–midnight

❶ *The colourful streets of Havana hold many small cafés*

Al Medina €€ **❼** (see page 17) In one of the oldest streets in the city, serving wonderful *mezzes*. Locals know to head upstairs for the same food (noon–16.00) at a fraction of the price. ⓐ Oficios e/ Plaza de Armas 🕒 Open noon–23.00

Meson de la Flota €€ **❽** (see page 17) Set menu in a rustic setting, with popular Flamenco shows at 13.00 and 20.00. ⓐ Mercaderes 257 ☎ (7) 863 3838

Monseigneur € **❾** (see page 22) An opulent, but intimate and inexpensive French restaurant with a history that dates back to the 1950s. Friendly staff and live piano music most nights. ⓐ Calle 21 e/ 'O' ☎ (7) 832 9884

Mulata del Sabor € **❿** (see page 17) This family-run *paladar* is a must. The owner, Justina, serves a simple but delicious menu with lots of love and smiles and she may even dance with you after the meal. ⓐ Sol 153A e/ Cuba ☎ (7) 867 5984 🕒 Open noon–midnight

Restaurant Paella €€ **⓫** (see page 17) A charming place inside Hostal Valencia with delicious Spanish cuisine and good wines, although surprisingly the paella is nothing special. ⓐ Calle de los Oficios 53 e/ Obrapía ☎ (7) 867 1037 🕒 Open noon–23.00

La Roca €€ **⓬** (see page 22) International and Creole cooking can be found here, in a cozy setting with live piano music and occasional stand-up comedy in Spanish. ⓐ Calle 21 102 e/ 'M' ☎ (7) 834 4501 🕒 Open noon–02.00

La Torre de Marfil € **⓭** (see page 17) Despite its ornate red and gold interior, this Chinese restaurant is not big on atmosphere, but the set meals, which include a drink, are great value. ⓐ Mercaderes e/ Obispo y Obrapía ☎ (7) 867 1038 🕒 Open noon–midnight

Torrelavega € **⓮** (*see page 17*) On a pretty, tree-filled square, with efficient service and decent portions. Go for breakfast or the cheap, set meal. ❷ Calle Obrapía e/ Oficios 🕒 Open 09.00–21.00

NIGHTLIFE

Much of the focus for nightlife in Havana is in its larger hotels, all of which have bars. Many of these offer entertainment in the form of cabarets and discos, but there are plenty of other atmospheric bars in the city and in the nearby suburb of Marianao, where world-class musicians and dancers perform for tips.

Nightclubs change quickly, so it is best to ask around for the latest information. Things usually don't get going until around midnight, so make sure you don't peak too early.

The Tropicana Cabaret **⓯** (*see page 22*) Takes place under the stars on an impressive estate, that dates back to Havana's glory days in the 1930s. ❷ Calle 72, 4505 e/41 y 45, Marianao ❶ (7) 267 1717 🕒 Admission from 21.00, show starts at 22.00 ❶ Reservations in advance, either direct or from most hotel receptions, and conservative dress is required.

Cabaret Parisien **⓰** (*see page 22*) More reasonably priced and at the Hotel Nacional, this is all you'd expect, with dancing girls and lots of frills, but few surprises. You can choose to have a buffet (served in the restaurant before the show) or dinner at your table in the run up to the cabaret. ❷ Calle 21 y 0 ❶ (7) 333 564 🕒 Show starts at 22.00 (arrive from 21.00) and finishes at midnight; after the cabaret, a live band will entertain you until 03.00.

BAR CRAWL

You could also go on a bar crawl of Ernest Hemingway's old haunts, sampling mojitos and daiquiris – the two cocktails that 'Papa', as he was known, drank to excess:

La Bodeguita del Medio ❼ (*see page 17*) This bar is probably the most famous Hemingway hangout. ❸ Empedrado 207, near Plaza de la Cathedral 🕐 Open 11.00–midnight

El Floridita ❽ (*see page 17*) Famous for being the birthplace of the daiquiri, Hemingway was often to be seen propping up the bar. But don't bother eating at the overpriced, mediocre restaurant. ❸ Obispo 557 🕐 Open 11.00–midnight

Be warned – Hemingway's watering holes are very much on the tourist trail. Prices are high and you won't be drinking with Cubans.

Casa de la Musica ❾ (*see page 22*) A friendly mix of Cubans and foreign tourists here, whether sharing a table and a bottle of rum, or getting down on the large dance floor. Get there early, as around midnight the superb live music gives way to pre-recorded Europop. ❸ Galliano y Concordia ❶ (7) 862 4165 🕐 Open 22.00–02.00 ❶ There is also a sister club located at Calle 20, 3308 e/ 35 in the exclusive Miramar neighbourhood.

Habana Club ❿ (*see page 17*) This is an established disco, where the clientele is mostly over 30. ❸ Calle 3ra e/ 86, Miramar ❶ (7) 204 2902 🕐 Opening hours are unpredictable

La Mina ❶ (*see page 17*) If you feel the need for a quiet, late-night drink, the chilled-out staff at this bar will serve you a fine mojito at any hour. Their patio bar is a great place to catch up with late-night stragglers, although the resident pair of peacocks might be sound asleep. During the day, pop around the corner to La Mina's great ice cream parlour. ❸ Plaza de Armas

Varadero
exclusive resort

The country's principal resort, strung out along 19 km (12 miles) of the Península de Hicacos, has always been an elitist spot. From the early days of the 20th century until the Revolution, it formed a playground for wealthy North Americans. Varadero was a place for them to find sun and rum, and indulge their vices to excess. In the 1930s, the American millionaire Du Pont risked most of his personal fortune by buying up almost all the peninsula north of Varadero. He built himself a mansion, golf course, yacht club and airstrip. Others followed, including mafia boss Al Capone, who had a summer house here.

The party ended when Batista fled the country and a victorious Castro rode into Havana. The sumptuous homes were reclaimed by the state and the beaches were made public in 1959.

Today, tourists are sheltered from the realities of everyday life as Cubans are mostly excluded from the whole peninsula. Despite the overwhelming number of modern hotels, there are pockets of history here. Historic buildings include a few simple wooden houses dating from the end of the 19th century that were once home to rich planters, and the 1950s **Hotel Internacional**, where gangsters held court in the casino and swimming pool.

THINGS TO SEE & DO
Parque Josone ★★★
A visit to this park where families gather at weekends, gives a glimpse of real Cuban life. Take a rowing boat out on the lake surrounded by artificial hills and populated by exotic plants and birds, or sit and watch the world go by in one of the many bars and restaurants. ② Avenida 1ra y Calle 56

Museo Municipal ★
You could just look at this museum from the outside, as its best feature is simply the mansion itself, built in 1929. A balcony looks out over the

landscaped gardens to the sea beyond. Inside, there are Indian artefacts and English-language exhibits telling the story of Varadero. ⓐ Calle 57 y Ave 1ra ⓣ (45) 613 189 ⓛ Open Tues–Sun

Varasub ★★★

Great for children, these 90-minute tours on a glass-bottomed boat are a relaxing way to experience the treasures of the local waters without getting your feet wet. Hotel receptions and agencies can provide details. ⓐ Super Clubs Puntarenas, West Varadero ⓛ Departures several times daily

Tours of the Peninsula ★★

Explore this green finger of land by bicycle, scooter, or even horse-drawn carriage. Although there are many holiday complexes, shops and restaurants here, they are surrounded by colourful bougainvillea, red and orange royal poinciana, aptly named 'flamboyant trees', and elegant palms.

Du Pont Mansion ★★★

This three-story villa is now a French restaurant, Las Américas (see page 45), but non-diners can visit for a small charge. Way back in 1926, Du Pont commissioned the two Cuban architects responsible for Havana's spectacular El Capitolio (see page 23) to create his own private paradise

on the rocks of San Bernardino, the highest point in Varadero. With its plush interior, exotic garden and even a golf course, the indulgent venture cost a small fortune. When he fled, the whole estate was nationalized and the villa became a state-run restaurant a few years later. ⓐ Avenida Las Américas, Reparto Las Torres ❶ (45) 667 750

Delfinario ★★
Here, trained dolphins in captivity perform three times a day, and you can pay extra to swim with them. ⓐ Autopista Sur (5 km/3 miles north-east of Du Pont Mansion) ❶ (45) 668 031 ⏱ Open 09.00–17.00

Cueva de Ambrosio ★★
This limestone cave was only discovered in 1961. It features around 50 prehistoric paintings, although some drawings may also have been created by African slaves. ⓐ Autopista Sur, 500 m (547 yds) east of Club Amigo Varadero ⏱ Open 09.00–16.30

Punta Hicacos ★★
The deserted, far-eastern part of the peninsula forms a national park that includes walking trails, an enormous cactus known as El Patriarca, and Laguna Mangón. However, the highlight is undoubtably the beach of Las Calaveras, with its mile upon mile of mostly deserted sand.

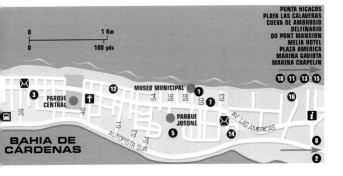

Cayos Piedras del Norte ★★

An artificial, underwater playground for divers and glass-bottomed boat
passengers has been created by sinking vessels such as a yacht,
a frigate and a towboat, as well as various missiles and a plane.
ⓐ 5 km (3 miles) north of Playa Las Calaveras

BEACH

Varadero's main attraction is the seemingly endless beach of white sand
that is cleaned every day. Avenida Primera runs along the northern coast
of the peninsula and becomes Avenida Las Américas to the east, which is
where you will find most of the larger hotels and yacht clubs. Generally,
the further east you travel along the finger of land, the more upmarket
it becomes. A motorway runs along the southern side.

EXCURSIONS

Seafari Cayo Blanco ★★★

This highly recommended catamaran day trip takes in the Delfinario
and includes an open bar, lunch on Cayo Blanco, snorkelling and a
sunset cruise.

Jungle tour ★★★

A half-day trip on two-person jet-skis through mangroves on the south
coast of Varadero, where you may see wildlife and can possibly even hug
a crocodile. ⓐ Aquaworld Marina Chapelin ⓣ (45) 667 550

Scuba diving ★

Around 30 dive sites dot the area, including Cayos Piedras del Norte
and underwater caves. The only dive from shore is at Playa Coral, 20 km
(12 miles) from Varadero; the rest are boat dives. Snorkellers can join
diving groups for a lower fee.

ⓞ *Varadero beach tour – a popular way to view the area*

◯ *Grilled lobster is usually on several beach restaurant menus in Varadero*

Skydiving ★★★

Thrill-seekers can jump 3000m (9842 ft) from a copy of a WWII biplane in tandem with an instructor. An initial 30 seconds of adrenaline-inducing free-fall is followed by a gentle, 10-minute float down to the beach. Ultralight flights are also available. ❸ Centro Internacional de Paracaidismo, old airport, opposite Marina Acua ❶ (45) 667 256

> ↘ Skydiving is only safe under certain weather conditions, for which you may have to wait several days. If you think you might like to try this activity, start enquiring as soon as you arrive in the resort.

Deep-sea fishing ★

Half- or one-day trips are possible from all of the resort's three marinas: Marina Chapelín, Marina Gaviota and Marina Acua. Enquire at your hotel for more information; transfers are normally provided.

Cuevas de Bellamar ★★

Half-day tours to these caves near Matanzas include lunch and optional horse riding and snorkelling.

If you are in a group of four or more, you can usually arrange to go on a private tour (avoiding big bus groups) for only a small extra charge.

RESTAURANTS (see map on pages 40–41)

Most of the hotel resorts are all-inclusive and provide buffets, along with a choice of several restaurants, often with themes. Private restaurants have been banned, and the big international hotels have monopolized much of the eating scene, making authentic, Cuban dining experiences hard to come by. Locals in the street may offer to cook you a lobster supper in their house. If this appeals, it is not a bad idea to establish what you are getting for your money. Such suppers are a matter of pot-luck, but are usually worth it for the experience of meeting a local family, if not for the food itself.

 Albacora €€ ❶ Wonderfully fresh fish and seafood are on the menu at this upmarket beachside restaurant. ❷ Calle 59 y Avenida 1ra ❶ (45) 613 650

Las Américas €€€ ❷ French and international food is served to tourists in elegant surroundings in one of the most expensive restaurants in Varadero. ❷ Du Pont Mansion, Autopista Sur Km 8.5 ❶ (45) 667 750 ❶ Reservations recommended

It is cheaper to eat in the arcade at the Du Pont Mansion, rather than in the restaurant itself. If you don't want to fork out for dinner here, you could just drop by for an early evening cocktail.

El Bodegón Criollo €€ ❸ Modelled on the famous La Bodequita del Medio in Havana, this is one of the few places in Varadero specializing in Cuban cuisine. There are lovely beach views and the set meals are great value. ⓐ Ave 1ra y Calle 40

La Brasas €€ ❹ Creole dishes, including barbecued pork and beef. ⓐ Camino del Mar y Calle 12 ⓒ Open noon– midnight

Parque Josone € ❺ Fast-food places, serving slices of pizzas and hot dogs, will fill the stomach, if nothing else. Otherwise, try the Italian waterside eatery, Dante. ⓐ Avenida 1ra y 56 ⓣ (45) 667 738 ⓒ Open 11.00–23.00

Pizza Nova € ❻ Reliable pizza outlet that even delivers. ⓐ Av 1 e/ Calle 13 ⓣ (45) 614 806 ⓒ Open 10.00–midnight

Restaurante La Fondue €€ ❼ For a change, try beef and fondue at this very good French-Swiss restaurant. ⓐ Avenida I y Calle 62, opposite Hotel Cuatro Palmas ⓣ (45) 667 747 ⓒ Open noon– midnight

NIGHTLIFE

Piano bars can be found in most of the larger hotels, most of which are open 24 hours, such as **Bar Las Américas** ❽ (ⓐ Melia Hotel Las Américas on the avenue of the same name). **Bar Beny** ❾ (ⓐ Camino del Mar y Calle 12) is a relaxed beach bar and with generally good, jazz-influenced music. **Bar Mirador** ❿ (ⓐ on the upper floor of the Du Pont Mansion) is recommended for a sunset cocktail.

◀ *Cuban nightlife in full colour*

La Cueva del Pirata ⓫ (ⓐ Autopista Sur Km 11) has a show and disco every night in a cave, while **El Kastillito Club ⓬** (ⓐ Av de la Playa e Calle 49) is a large, modern nightclub. Both are packed with tourists, but you might spot a local or two. **Club Mambo ⓭** (ⓐ Avenida Las Américas next to Club Amigo Varadero) attracts a fashionable crowd. **Discoteca Havana Club ⓮** (ⓐ Avenida 3 y Calle 62) is loud and brash, and again is visited mostly by tourists.

The historic cabarets in Havana are well worth a visit (see page 37). **Habana Café ⓯** has a cabaret and disco (ⓐ Avenida Las Américas) with a slick show followed by a disco that tends to attract an older crowd. On the same street a few blocks west, another cabaret and disco takes place from Tuesday to Sunday at **Cabaret Continental ⓰** (ⓐ Hotel Internacional), with dinner an optional extra. **Parque Josone** (ⓐ Avenida 1ra and Calle 58) has shows for tourists with Cuban singing and dancing which usually take place at 21.00 on Fridays and Saturdays. Ask at your hotel for the latest details.

If you have teenage children, some clubs put on Sunday afternoon discos for youngsters, which are popular with Cubans.

SHOPPING

All the large hotels have shops mostly selling t-shirts, souvenirs and cigars at higher prices than other outlets. At **Parque Central** (ⓐ Avenida 1ra, between Calles 44 and 46) local artisans sell their wares to visitors. In fact, much of Avenida 1ra, between the Laguna and Parque Josone, is lined with small market stalls, where leather goods are a particularly good buy. **Casa del Habano** on Avenida 1ra y Calle 31 is a good bet for world-famous Cuban cigars. Service is good here and you can even see the cigars being rolled. **Plaza América** is one of Varadero's largest shopping centre, selling clothes, music, shoes and souvenirs, and is also home to a bank and post office.

⬥ *Markets are a treasure trove of Cuban delights*

Cayo Largo
sun-kissed paradise

With a wide selection of heavenly beaches and great weather all year round, this small island has become one of Cuba's most popular holiday destinations. Lying 80 km (50 miles) south of the Bay of Pigs, the island offers everything you could want from a holiday in Cuba, except contact with ordinary Cubans (which is why many try to combine their holiday here with a few nights in Havana). The resorts and facilities here are among the best in Cuba, the reef dives are breathtaking, and this is one of the few places in Cuba where you can work on an all-over tan.

THINGS TO SEE & DO

If you're staying at one of the Sol Meliá hotels (e.g. Sol Club, the Linda Arena or the Pelícano) you can use the facilities of any of their other hotels. The same applies to Gran Caribe, which runs the Isla del Sur and Lindamar. Both groups are building more hotels, and this deal can mean

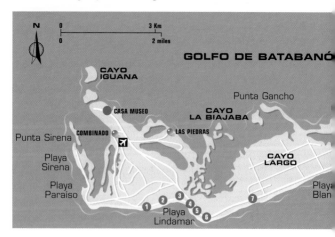

that your all-inclusive holiday has a little more variety from day to day – kids, in particular, will enjoy trying out the full range of pools and games rooms available to them. Other than hotel activities, it's mainly about the sun, sea and sand.

Sailing & snorkelling ★ ★ ★

A relaxing way to reach the reef is by sailing boat, which you can arrange (with or without crew) through your hotel. Bring along snorkelling gear for a close-up of the colourful world beneath the waves, but ask if the currents are safe first, as swimmers have occasionally been driven onto the jagged reefs. If you fancy working up a sweat, kayaks and pedalos are available at most of the hotels.

Riding or cycling ★ ★

The beaches away from the big hotels can easily be reached by hiring a bicycle, or by going on horseback, and both are great ways to seek out a special, secluded spot. One hotel in each of the groups usually serves as a rental centre, so just ask at reception.

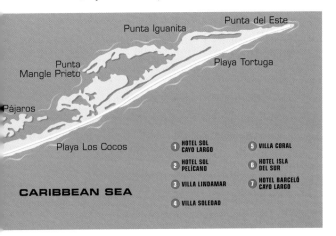

Punta del Este

Punta Iguanita

Punta Mangle Prieto

Playa Tortuga

Pájaros

Playa Los Cocos

CARIBBEAN SEA

1 HOTEL SOL CAYO LARGO
2 HOTEL SOL PELÍCANO
3 VILLA LINDAMAR
4 VILLA SOLEDAD
5 VILLA CORAL
6 HOTEL ISLA DEL SUR
7 HOTEL BARCELÓ CAYO LARGO

Scuba diving ★

Cayo Largo's stunning coral reefs are ideal for experienced divers, but also for beginners looking for certification. There are plenty of qualified, English-speaking instructors who will coach you through the basics, often with a gentle introduction in the hotel swimming pool.

Nature tours ★

Visit the marine sanctuary at Combinado and see the turtles that are bred there, or just grab your binoculars and spot the hummingbirds, flamingos and countless other bird species that inhabit the island.

BEACHES

Like the famous, white sandy beaches, or *playas blancas*, of Cancún, the grains of 'sand' here are formed by crushed coral rather than rock, so it stays cool underfoot. **Playa Lindamar** is a 5 km (3 mile) stretch of sheltered beach on the south coast of the island that is home to a number of holiday complexes. North-east is **Playa Blanca**, the island's longest beach, and with the best facilities for tourists. In comparison, **Playa Sirena** on the extreme west of the island is an oasis of scenic calm. Nearby **Playa Paraíso** is a secluded spot, popular with topless and nude sunbathers. North-west of the large hotels and past Playa Blanca is **Los Cocos**, a dream of a beach with calm, shallow waters that are perfect for children. Further on is **Playa Tortuga**, a nesting spot for turtles. Be careful with warning flags on the beaches. As in other countries, red means swimming is dangerous and not allowed.

 Beaches in Cayo Largo offer little or no shade, so keep topped up on sun-protection lotion, wear a hat and drink plenty of water.

EXCURSIONS
Cayo Iguana ★★★

Home to a large iguana colony, these fleet-of-foot lizards have not yet learned to fear humans, offering a great chance to see the fascinating creatures close up. Organized boat trips are available from most hotels.

Fishing ★★★

Take to the seas and test your cunning against marlin, swordfish and snapper. The boats all have experienced crew who will take you to the best locations. Details at Hotel Isla del Sur or the Meliá Arena.

Islands Beach Tour ★★★

This traditional boat cruise, with lunch and visits to out-of-the way beaches is popular. The beach on **Cayo Rico** is stunning.

RESTAURANTS & BARS

Most holidaymakers will insist that their all-inclusive hotel has a restaurant and bar, but do check, as some here do not – hence the need to allow access to other hotels in the group. For decent pasta and pizza, head to **Villa Lindamar**. The Meliá group hotels are generally more upmarket and offer a wider selection of in-house dining options. You will be able to choose from buffets, steaks, pizza, Cuban specialities and fine international dining as well as all the comforts of home.

NIGHTLIFE

With free drinks, planned entertainment and discos on offer at your hotel, you may not may not feel like straying too far on a 'night out'. For true disco lovers, there is a minibus operating from 23.00 through to the early hours. This does the rounds of the hotel discos and also visits the **Blue Iguana** nightclub near the airport. The nightclub at the **Pelicano** is worth a look as many partygoers end up here; or for something a little more exclusive, try the **Linda Arena**.

SHOPPING

 Each hotel is equipped with one or more *tiendas* (shops) where you can stock up on souvenirs, snacks, cigars, cigarettes and more, or you can visit the tiny shopping centre at Isla del Sur. Diehard shoppers may consider a day trip to Havana.

RESORTS

Cayo Coco & Cayo Guillermo
Islands in the stream

If you are in search of an idyllic beach holiday, look no further than the two cayos. Just off the north coast of Cuba, there are around 400 islands in the Jardines del Rey (Gardens of the King) archipelago. Almost all are uninhabited, but on Cayo Coco there are plenty of hotels, miles of fine beach and even an international airport. Inland, the island is thick with forest and jungle, which gives way further south to swampy mangroves that are home to a teeming variety of wildlife.

A 27 km (17 mile) long causeway links Coco to the mainland. The Cubans who work in the hotels here make their way back along this road every day, as they are not allowed to live on the island.

To the west of Cayo Coco, and connected to it by another causeway, is the much smaller island of Cayo Guillermo. The diving here is world-class and so is the fishing – which is probably why the cayos get an honourable mention in Hemingway's book, *Islands in the Stream*. In both the cayos, you can pay in CUCs (Cuban Convertible Pesos) or euros.

THINGS TO SEE & DO
During the day, the all-inclusive hotels lay on plenty of guest activities, most of them centred on the pool and poolside bar. There may be a quieter, adult-only pool away from the fun and games, and most places have a crèche for toddlers, a kids' club and a games room. More hotels are being built every year, and the activity list is growing, with tennis courts, gyms, saunas and beauty spas becoming more commonplace.

Sitio La Güira ★ ★
Visit this farm and see an odd assortment of performing animals, among them a ladder-climbing poodle and an 'ox on a box'. There is also a bar and restaurant here (see page 63).

Water sports ★★★

Every hotel here has a water sports centre, where you can arrange windsurfing lessons, or just head off to explore in a sea kayak or pedalo. Water-skiers are well catered for at most hotels, and lessons can be arranged for beginners.

Budding powerboat racers can take control of their own speedboat for a *Miami Vice*-style sprint through the swampy everglades on the south coast of Cayo Coco. An experienced guide leads a convoy of two or three boats.

Parque Natural El Bagá ★★★

This nature reserve is a mixture of mangroves, lagoons, jungle and forest trails, this park makes an ideal spot for hiking or horse-riding tours.

Cueva del Jabali ★★

The daily magic shows and scary bats in this cave will keep the kids entertained, and the bar is open all day. ➌ Near the Melia Cayo Coco 🕐 Bar open 10.00–16.00; restaurant open 10.00–late

Eco-Safari ★★

Jump in a jeep and be whisked off to La Redonda Lake for a boat tour. A trip to the crocodile farm is followed by a one-hour trek on horseback. The tour includes lunch at Sito La Güira.

Snorkelling & diving ★★★

One of the biggest coral reefs in the world is on your doorstep here, so don't miss out. Offshore, the reef depth varies between 5 m (16 ft) and 40 m (130 ft) and the water is crystal clear. You can see parrotfish, yellowtail snapper, angel fish, anemones and spiny lobsters, together with a colourful variety of underwater plants.

Week-long dive course with international accreditation can be booked through **Blue Diving** ➓ Hotel Meliá Cayo Coco ☎ (33) 308 180 or at your hotel. Beginners can take a morning introductory course in the hotel pool. There are another two dive centres on Cayo Guillermo,

⬥ *Cayo Coco hotel swimming pool*

◯ A Cayo Coco bridge crosses over to the white coral beach

Marinas Puertosol ➋ Villa Océano ➊ (33) 301 738 and Cubanacán
Náutica ➋ Hotel Meliá Cayo Guillermo ➊ (33) 301 627

Bird watching ★

Cayo Coco is named, not after the coconuts that are everywhere, but
after the white (*coco* in Spanish) ibis bird. The islands are home to over
200 bird species, including a colony of over 30,000 roseate flamingos.

BEACHES

The spotless, white coral beaches of Cayo Coco run in an almost continu-
ous strip along the north coast. Not surprisingly, this is where all the
hotels are, so no matter which one you are in, you are guaranteed a fine
spot close by. The Hotel Senador (rumoured to be in the midst of a
Sandals takeover) offers good access for visitors with disabilities, right
onto the sands. **Playa Flamencos** is good for swimming and you can go
horse riding along the sands here too. **La Jaula** is a nice quiet spot, as is
Playa Prohibida.

Over on Guillermo is perhaps the best beach of the lot, **Playa Pilar**,
named after Hemingway's fishing boat, *Pilar*. This is also one of the few
beaches not yet snapped up by a hotel. Kids will love the 15 m (16½ yds)
high sand dunes behind the fine stretch of beach.

EXCURSIONS

All the excursions below can be booked through the Cubanacán and
Cubatour desks, which are found in almost all the hotels.

Sugar Mill Trip ★

Take a speedboat ride across a lake and through a mangrove swamp,
then visit a crocodile farm where you can get up close and personal... at
least to the baby crocs. After a traditional Cuban lunch, climb aboard a
steam train for a ride through sugar cane fields, take a tour of a working
sugar mill, and then go on a horse-and-cart ride through the nearby
town of Morón. The trip lasts around six hours, but departures times and
cost are subject to change, so ask at the Cubanacán desk in your hotel.

⬥ *There are plenty of water sports, including sailing, on offer at Cayo Guillermo*

Hop to Havana ★★★

A popular (but pricey) expedition with those who have not pre-booked a stopover in the capital is this one-day flight tour to Havana. It takes in key sites such as the Plaza de Armas (see page 19), the El Morro castle and El Capitolio (see page 23). You can also choose to stay overnight, in which case you will be treated to the spectacular cabaret at the famous outdoor Tropicana nightclub (see page 37).

Catamaran Trip ★★

Spend the day relaxing, topping up your tan and cooling down with the odd dip, as the crew of the boat whisk you around a selection of beaches and colourful reefs.

Fishing ★

Those interested in sport-fishing should head to the Marina Puertosol in Cayo Guillermo. Day trips for smaller catches are popular, or you can opt for three-day expeditions and hunt big sailfish. Laguna La Redonda is home to many species of freshwater fish and is a well-known international bass fishing site.

Trinidad & tower ★★

Take a trip to Trinidad and visit the slave watchtower (see page 75) at Manaca Inzaga. The coach will pick you up from your resort and bring you back the same day, or you can opt for an overnight tour with a night in Cienfuegos and a visit to Che Guevara's last resting place in Santa Clara (see page 81).

RESTAURANTS (see map on page 54)

Hotel Dining €–€€ Most hotels offer a range of dining options, from basic buffets to fine dining, taking in steaks, pizza and pasta along the way. You will usually find a Cuban restaurant, too. Although most of these will be included in your package, you may need to pay extra for the 'VIP' restaurants, and reservations and smart dress might be required.

Beach Bars € Outside of the all-inclusive hotels, your options are limited. On Cayo Coco, there is a beach bar in front of the Senador serving basic, fried fish dishes, and another near the Hotel Tryp Coco.

 La Sila € ❶ The location is not great and it lacks atmosphere, but the food is okay. ❸ On the causeway to the mainland.
🕒 Open 10.00–21.00

 Sitio La Güira €€ ❷ This farm restaurant does decent lunches and powerful cocktails. 🕒 Open 10.00–22.00

NIGHTLIFE

Most hotels put on a different cabaret-style show each night (usually rotated on a 14-day basis), and after that there are the discos, which, given the captive audience, tend to be lively affairs. Ask at your hotel if you can visit other hotel bars and discos with your armband (some Melia hotels, for example, allow this). **The Cueva del Jabali**, near the Melia Cayo Coco is a natural cave that operates as a bar and disco. All the hotels run mini-tours here. Another popular spot is the open-air bar at **Sitio La Güira** bar, which gets going around midnight.

 Don't be tempted by a shopping trip to Morón, which lies 50 km (31 miles) to the south across the causeway – there is even less to buy here than on the cayos.

 SHOPPING
Keen souvenir hunters may consider a day-trip to Havana. On the two cayos, it's Che t-shirts, cigars and rum, and not much else. All the hotels have a souvenir shop and another shop selling cigarettes, alcohol and magazines (although none of them will be British and few will be written in English).

MUSEO CHORRO
DE MAITA, BANES

Guardalavaca
Village

Playa Guardalavaca

CENTRO COMERCIAL
LOS FLAMBOYANES

HANDICRAFT
MARKET

CENTRO COMERCIAL
GUARDALAVACA

Agiada
La Piedra

Punta
Guardalavaca

HOLGUIN

Playa
Caletica

YACHT
ANCHORAGE

ATLANTIC
OCEAN

AQUARIUM

Playa
Esmeralda

CAYO
JUTÍA

LAS GUANAS
ECO-ARCHAEOLOGICAL
TRAIL

BAHIA DE
NARANJO

N

0   1 km
0   0.5 miles

1 HOTEL LAS
   BRISAS

2 VILLA LAS
   BRISAS

3 HOTEL
   GUARDALAVACA

4 CLUB AMIGO
   ATLÁNTICO Y
   BUNGALOWS

5 VILLA CABAÑAS

6 PARADISUS
   RIO DE ORA

7 SOL CLUB
   RIO DE LUNA

8 MELIÁ RIO
   DE MARES

9 BUNGALOW
   BIRANCITO

Guardalavaca
Relaxed retreat

This modern resort, built in the mid-1980s, is made up of a handful of all-inclusive hotel complexes that are a world away from everyday Cuban life. These international retreats are designed to meet all your needs, from eating to entertainment. Just 56 km (35 miles) from Holguín's international airport, Guardalavaca sits in an unspoilt, scenic area of green rolling hills, and manages to retain a peaceful atmosphere. Its name means 'watch the cow', after the skinny egrets that follow cattle around in search of the flies that follow the cows. Bahía de Naranjo includes a 32 km (20 mile) stretch of coastline, as well as lush hillsides and woodland and three tiny islands within easy reach of the mainland.

THINGS TO SEE & DO
Hotel activities ★
All of the big hotels here have a programme of activities, so you need never be bored. There may be games by the pool, a gym and even tennis courts. Kid's clubs are aimed to keep youngsters occupied.

Water sports ★
Kayaking and windsurfing, as well as snorkelling, can be arranged from most beaches.

Cayo Naranjo Aquarium ★★★
Dolphin and sea lion shows at this aquarium on a nearby island in the bay are best visited on a boat tour around the Bay of Naranjo. Ask at your hotel for details.

Take a ride ★★
Travel back in time in a traditional horse-drawn carriage, either between Playa Esmeralda and Playa Guardalavaca, or Playa Esmeralda and Bahía de Naranjo. Alternatively, charter one for half an hour or more, and go your own way. Bicycle use is included in most hotel packages, and moped

◯ *Surf and sun at relaxing Guardalavaca*

hire is also possible. You can take a thrilling tandem sky-dive, or go on a more gentle Ultralight flight. Your hotel will be able to arrange this for you, along with transfers.

> Always agree on a price before getting into one of the horse-drawn carriages, or you could find yourself landed with a hefty bill. This rule also applies to taxis.

BEACHES

With turquoise water and sparkling white sand, the beaches here are a big draw. The aptly named **Playa Esmeralda** with its jade waters, lies a few miles west of Guardalavaca and is the main beach, dominated by three mammoth hotel complexes managed by Spain's Sol Meliá group. A coral reef running not far from the shore provides for spectacular snorkelling and diving.

EXCURSIONS

Museo Chorro de Maita ★★★

A world away from the slick tourist resorts, and just a few miles south of Guardalavaca, is the site of a native Indian village. An enormous cemetery was discovered here, along with more than 50 skeletons. It is worth the trip if only for its lovely, hilltop setting. ⓐ Cerro de Yaguajay ⓒ Open Tues–Sat 09.00–17.00

Banes ★★

A beautiful drive through scenic hills will take you to this country town, 32 km (20 miles) south-west of Holguín. Perfect for a glimpse of real Cuban life, Banes is also the centre of an important area of excavation. The adjacent **Museo Indocubano Bani** is a significant archaeological museum, second only to Havana's. There are around a thousand articles on display, ranging from knives and large terracotta vases to the tiny (only 5 cm/2 inches high) but symbolic Idolo de Oro, a 13th-century gold fertility figure of a woman, which was found nearby. ⓐ Calle General Marrero 305 y Marti ⓣ (24) 82487 ⓒ Open Tues–Sun 09.00–13.00

⬥ *Lush woodland surrounds a lake in Eastern Cuba*

Diving ★★

The area boasts more than 30 dive sites, almost all of which can only be reached by boat. There is plenty to interest underwater explorers here, including shipwrecks, coral reefs, caves and sea life of every shape, size and colour. Ask at your hotel for details.

RESTAURANTS (see map on page 64)

Almost all tourists in the area will have bought an all-inclusive deal in which all meals have been paid for. There are a handful of local, simple restaurants next to Guardalavaca beach, with authentic Cuban food and lots of fish and seafood.

El Cayuelo € ❶ A well-established, small beachside restaurant serving fish, lobster, paella and seafood. ⓐ 800 m (875 yds) east of Hotel Las Brisas, Playa Guardalavaca

Paradisus Rio de Oro €€ ❷ An upmarket, floating Japanese restaurant – a welcome change from the standard buffet and European food served in most hotels. ⓐ Carretera de Guardalavace, Playa Esmeralda ❶ (24) 30090

El Rápido €€ ❸ This Cuban chain restaurant may appeal to fast-food lovers. It is open around the clock for sandwiches, chicken and chips, and pizza. ❷ Centro Commercial Los Flamboyanes

---

Local restaurants tend to close early (around 21.00, or earlier if there are no customers) so don't leave it too late to eat.

NIGHTLIFE

All of the hotels have their own bar and disco; many also put on shows. One of the swankiest, **Paradisus Río de Oro** has a piano bar and 'Fun Pub', which is restricted to tourists. **Sol Río de Luna y Mares** has a beachside disco.

 Your armband may allow you to use the bar, restaurants and various other facilities in sister hotels in the same group, such as the Sol Meliá group.

SHOPPING

Touristy gift shops in all the hotels sell a mostly uninspiring selection of Che Guevara memorabilia, Cuban music CDs, t-shirts and souvenirs. However, **Casa del Habanos** in Centro Commercial Los Flamboyanes sells good-quality Cuban cigars.

EXCURSIONS
Out & about

Exploring Cuba

Cuba's treasures are a reflection of its rich cultural and natural heritage. Some are of world importance and recognized by UNESCO; others played a role in the Revolution and are not only nationally noteworthy, but part of the Cuban psyche. The low cost of internal airfares means that most locations in Cuba are easily accessible, even on a day trip. You may choose to take an organized tour for convenience, or go it alone by making arrangements yourself and possibly hiring a car (see page 114).

Old Havana with its Spanish-built fortifications and the green Valley of Viñales are UNESCO World Heritage Sites that cannot fail to delight. Trinidad, with its pretty colonial houses and museums is a world apart from the capital, but only five hours' drive away. The atmospheric town and nearby Valle de los Ingenios, with its fascinating sugar plantations, are also World Heritage Sites and make for popular excursions. Pockets of 'Revolutionary Cuba' are found far and wide, with highlights in Havana, The Bay of Pigs and Santiago de Cuba. Not just for those with a special interest in the country's history, these special places offer an insight to the hearts and minds of the Cuban people.

HAVANA BY DAY (AND NIGHT!)

If your Cuban package doesn't include a couple of nights in Havana – and many do – it is well worth the visit to this wonderful, world-famous city (see page 16). Although many of the buildings have seen better days, it is still a real architectural gem, with a unique buzz generated by the many bars and restaurants where live music is usually on the menu. Then there are the exotic cabaret shows at the **Hotel Nacional** (see page 27), the famous outdoor **Tropicana** (see page 37) and, of course, the ever-friendly and party-loving Havanaros, as the city's residents are called.

Day and overnight coach trips from Varadero can be booked from your hotel. From Cayo Coco and Guillermo, you can take a one-day flight tour that includes some key attractions, or you can choose to stay overnight and sample the nightlife as well. Flight tours also leave from Guardalavaca and Cayo Largo.

If you decide to go your own way and not take a city tour, make sure not to miss **El Capitolio** (see page 23), a near-copy of America's seat of government. Also be sure to visit the historic centre of Havana in **Plaza de Armas** (see page 19) and the impressive **El Morro Castle** (see page 20), built by the Spanish to ward off pirates. Apart from the traditional cabarets, there is plenty to keep you entertained at night, from **Hemingway haunts** to lively discos (see pages 37–38).

VALLEY OF VIÑALES

Extraordinary, ancient rounded rocks called mogotes, fittingly known as 'elephant backs' by locals, lie in the west of the country. Cloaked in dense vegetation, they rise dramatically out of flat, green plains. Here, nature has sculpted the limestone landscape to form enormous caves and deep, underground rivers. The region is blanketed by pine forests, sugar cane fields, and even paddy fields, which are more reminiscent of Asia than Cuba. **Cueva del Indio** is a cave and artificially lit underground river, best visited by foot and then by motorboat.

◐ *Cuban buildings – faded, but architectural gems*

🔺 *A Trinidad horseman strolls through the town*

The Valley of Viñales can be visited on a day trip from Havana, although you will probably find yourself wanting more time. If you do get the chance to stay longer than a day, riding, cycling and walking explorations are all possible.

TRINIDAD

The peace of this quiet, colonial town is disturbed only by the occasional horseman riding through the cobblestone streets and regular bus loads of tourists (though they don't stay for long). If time seems to have stood still here, it is because for a while at least, it did. Trinidad thrived in the early 19th century when an influx of French refugees, fleeing a Slave Rebellion in Haiti, set up numerous sugar mills in the area. The two wars of independence halted the town's growth and by the mid-19th century, the town was once again a backwater.

The grand houses of the rich on Plaza Mayor have become museums, such as the **Museo Arquitectura Colonial** (☎ (419) 3208 ⏱ Open Mon–Sat 09.00–17.00). This 18th-century mansion once owned by a sugar magnate has its own fascinating architectural elements, but also illustrates the history of domestic 18th- and 19th-century architecture. The exquisite Casa de Aldemán Oritz was the former mayor's mansion, built in 1809 and now the **Galería de Arte**, with paintings for sale by Cuban artists as well as jewellery and pottery. Just off Plaza Mayor, the **Museo Histórico Municipal** (⌖ Simón Bolívar 423 ☎ (419) 4460) is a neo-classical mansion, also known as **Casa Cantero**, after its owner, a rich German planter who, it is rumoured, killed an old slave trader and married his widow, who died in mysterious circumstances shortly after the wedding. Don't miss the great views from the top of the tower here.

Trinidad has a confusing layout which some say was designed to disorient looting pirates. Today, it has the same effect on tourists. What makes matters worse is that most of its streets have two names!

🔺 *A sweeping view over Valle de los Ingenios*

VALLE DE LOS INGENIOS

Seven miles from Trinidad, the lush valley known as Valle de los Ingenios is dotted with 70 small, 19th-century *ingenios* (sugar mills), as well as historical machinery, slave huts and manor houses. The landscape of

green rolling hills and sugarcane fields, punctuated by towering Royal Palms, can be explored by steam train. Its focus is the Manaca Iznaga estate (❷ Km 16 Carretera de Sancti Spíritus ❶ (419) 4121 ❻ Open Tues–Sun 09.00–17.00) with a 44 m (144 foot) tower, built in 1830 by a showy landowner to keep an eye on the slaves working his plantation.

> **A BITE TO EAT**
>
> An elegant restaurant in the former plantation owner's lovely house on the Manaca Iznaga estate (see details on page 77) serves a small selection of dishes, such as pork casserole and chicken and rice. It is a charming spot for lunch on the terrace, accompanied by live music, but you will be surrounded by plenty of tourists from big tour groups.

If there are not enough people to make up a tour, it will be cancelled at the last minute. Why not get a few like-minded friends together and book as a group? That way, you will enjoy a more intimate experience for only a little more cash.

PARQUE BACONAO & SURROUNDS

This area, east of Santiago de Cuba and lying between the dramatic peaks of the Sierra Maestra and the Caribbean coast, can easily be explored by car in a day trip. East along the coast are a number of child-friendly attractions. **Valle de la Prehistoria** (ⓐ Carretera Baconao Km 6.5 ⓘ (63) 9039 ⓛ Open 08.00–18.00) features life-size, concrete dinosaurs and cave people, built by inmates of a nearby prison. Also here is the **Museo de Historia Natural**, although children may find it dull in comparison to the prehistoric monsters. Boat trips are possible on **Laguna Baconao** (where there is a small, lakeside crocodile farm) and along the scenic **Baconao River**. Sharks and sea lions can be seen from a viewing tunnel at the quite basic **Acuario Baconao** (ⓐ Km 27.5 ⓘ (31) 5156). Dolphins perform three times a day here, and you can also pay extra to swim with the captive animals. Inland, and out of the park area, is the spectacular 1214 m (4000 foot) extinct volcano of **Gran Piedra**, from where glimpses of Jamaica and Haiti can be had on a clear day. A short walk from here is the manor house and pine-covered plantations of **Cafetal La Isabelica** (ⓐ Carretera de la Gran Piedra Km 14 ⓛ Open Mon only) named after a French landowner's mistress.

Granjita Siboney (📍 Carretera Siboney Km 13.5 ☎ (63) 9168) at the western entrance to the park, is worth a visit only if you are passing. The farmhouse was used as a base to launch the failed Moncada Barracks attack (see page 82) and features reconstructed bullet holes, a museum with personal affects and the car Castro used in the attack. An adjoining gallery contains photographs and paintings in honour of those who died.

BARACOA & SURROUNDS

When Columbus stumbled across Baracoa, it quickly became a Spanish settlement and the country's first capital (albeit for just three years). Tucked away on Cuba's eastern corner, this lovely, sleepy town could only be accessed by boat until the 1960s, when a road was built through the almost impenetrable mountains. Its rather run-down cathedral is sand-wiched between a few narrow streets. In much better condition is the **castle**, now a hotel and restaurant (see box, below) and with good views of the memorable **El Yunque mountain**.

The main reason for visiting Baracoa, however, is its tranquil surrounds. To the north-west, locals fish and swim in the **Toa River** and relax at the pretty **Maguana Beach**. To the east, gentle boat rides across the peaceful **Yumurí River** pass beneath tall canyon walls along the way.

Snails, called *polimitas*, live in this area. However, don't be tempted to buy locally crafted jewellery made from their brightly coloured, striped shells, as the creatures are now endangered and their purchase is not only immoral but illegal.

A BITE TO EAT

The restaurant in Hotel El Castillo (see above), formerly a castle, is good for a snack or a more formal dinner of creole dishes and sea crab. 📍 Calle Calixto García, Loma el Paraíso 🕐 Open 10.00–23.00

Revolutionary Cuba

One of the best ways to understand the history of the Revolution and its meaning to the Cuban people is to visit some of the key sites in the historic struggle. Some of the most important events in the island's history happened in small towns, villages and cities far removed from the picturesque centre of Old Havana. Most of the places listed below can be visited with organized tours from the big resorts, or if you are feeling adventurous, you could hire a car and make your own way.

🔺 *Che Guevara (far left) and Fidel Castro (far right) at Castillo de Farnes*

SANTA CLARA

The remains of Che Guevara, who was murdered in Bolivia at the behest of the CIA, were finally returned to Cuba in 1997, thirty years after his death. He now rests in Santa Clara, where an evocative mausoleum, monument and museum have been built in his honour – **Memorial 'Comandante' Ernesto Che Guevara**.

It was in Santa Clara that the decisive battle of the Revolution was fought. With just 300 guerillas, Che led an attack on the town and defeated 3,000 government troops – bad news for the dictator Batista, but even worse was to come. The next day, an armoured train carrying guns and government reinforcements was derailed and sacked at Santa Clara by Che's band of rebels. Two days later, on New Year's Eve 1959, a panicked Batista left the country, never to return.

REVOLUTIONARY HAVANA

Although the main battles of the Revolution were fought elsewhere, the capital played its part in Cuba's history. Visit the expansive **Plaza de la Revolución in Vedado** (see page 28) where Fidel and Che were feted with a huge victory parade a week after Batista fled.

After the speeches, the leaders headed to **Castillo de Farnes** (see 'A Bite to Eat in Havana', page 82) where the two of them put their feet up and relaxed with coffee (Fidel) and beers (Che). A photograph on the wall commemorates the occasion.

Nearby is the **Museo de la Revolución**, (see page 24), which proudly tells the tale of the country's ongoing struggle. It was also the site of an unsuccessful assassination attempt against Fulgencio Batista in March 1957. The exhibits provide a complete documentary and photographic account of the Cuban revolution and is a must for anyone with an interest in the revolution and a taste for history. Labels are in English and Spanish. Among the early successes was a literacy campaign that sent 300,000 students and teachers out into the countryside to teach reading and writing. In just over one year, they taught over one million *campesinos* (peasant farmers), and Cuba now has a higher rate of literacy than either the UK or US.

SANTIAGO DE CUBA

The fight against imperialism did not begin with Fidel, but with heroic fighters from Santiago such as Antonio Maceo (born in 1845), who fought for independence from the Spanish. Fittingly, it was in Santiago that Fidel launched a dramatic but doomed attack on Batista's troops, to signal the start of the Revolution in 1953. The battle took place at the **Moncada Barracks**, now part of the **Parque Histórico Abel Santamaria** (ⓐ Calle General Portuondo e/ Ave Libertadores ❶ (22) 624 119).

Of the 120 guerillas that took part, 55 were captured, tortured and killed, and afterwards Fidel himself was put on trial here. He conducted his own defence, and his famous 'history will absolve me' speech is now the stuff of Cuban legend. In the centre of Santiago is **Parque Céspedes**, named after the Cuban Republic's first president, who was ambushed and killed by the Spanish. Opposite the cathedral in this square is the **Ayuntamiento** (town hall). From the first-floor balcony of this building, on New Year's Day 1959, Castro made his first speech to the Cuban people after the successful Revolution.

> ### A BITE TO EAT IN HAVANA
> The **Castillo de Farnes** restaurant (see page 34) is a stone's throw from the Museo de la Revolución. The pavement café serves good snacks and drinks, or you can retire to the comfortable restaurant for something more substantial. ⓐ Calle Monserrate e/ Obrapía ❶ (7) 867 1030 ❶ Open noon–midnight

THE BAY OF PIGS

This overseas adventure is perhaps one of the most infamous under-taken by the United States. Two years of Castro's rule had made rich Cuban émigrés and US big business bristle at the moves towards nation-alization of large plantations, oil, gas and electricity. President Eisenhower had already given the go-ahead to a CIA plan to overthrow the Cuban leadership, and on 15 April 1961, civilian Cuban airports and

◭ *Parque Céspedes in the centre of Santiago*

military airbases were bombed by enemy aircraft flying the Cuban insignia. The next day, an invasion force of 70 battalions struck at Playa Girón and Playa Larga in the Zapata peninsula, south-west of Havana.

The Museo Girón tells this riveting story with detailed maps, copies of CIA plans captured from the invaders, and personal effects of those killed in the invasion. An intriguing, sometimes harrowing 15-minute film, uses contemporary footage to document the 72-hour struggle that ended in humiliating defeat for the invaders. Cuba demanded, and was paid, $US53 million in food and medicine to return the 1200 mercenaries captured – the first time the US government had been forced to pay war reparations. ➌ Playa Girón ❶ (459) 4122 ❶ Open 09.00–17.00 ❶ Guided tours are available for Spanish speakers

Food & drink

Due to economic restrictions, good food is harder to come by in Cuba. Thankfully, if you are on an all-inclusive holiday, this is not something you need to worry about, although of course it is part of the daily struggle for most locals. They have to depend on their ration books for their staples, and the limited availability of ingredients means that meals constantly have to be 'invented'. Most large resort hotels put on buffet meals, and the food on offer here is usually as good as, or even better than, that offered in expensive restaurants.

Service can be slow, however. What is on the menu depends on what deliveries have been made that day, and portions are often on the small side, with few of the trimmings we might expect. This is a Cuban reality, and while every effort has been made in this book to seek out the best options, a good meal every time cannot be guaranteed.

Cuban food is a mix of Spanish and Afro-Caribbean cuisine and is rarely spicy. Pork and chicken are the most commonly found meats, along with beef to a lesser extent. Rice, beans, plantains (a kind of savoury banana) and yucca (a fibrous root vegetable) are staples that accompany most meals. Fresh vegetables are hard to find, even at upmarket hotels. Although Cuba is an island, most natives regard fish as food for the poor. It is, however, a large export industry, and fish and lobster (which is sadly now endangered as a result of over fishing) can be found on the menus of many state-run restaurants.

Moros y Cristianos (Moors and Christians) is the name for black beans and rice, and **Congrí** is rice with red beans. **Ropa vieja**, which literally means 'old clothes', is shredded beef with onions and peppers. A **bocadito** is a sandwich – usually made of ham or cheese, or both. Desserts are sometimes hard to come by due to milk shortages; however, it is worth looking out for the delicious Cuban **helado** (ice cream).

◀ *Cuban food, a mix of Spanish and Afro-Caribbean cuisine, is rarely spicy*

COOKING METHODS
a la plancha Cooked in a frying pan
asado Roasted
empanizado Breaded
parradilla/grille On the grill
sofrito Cuban seasoning made by sautéeing onions, garlic and
  sweet peppers

Menu Decoder

aceituna(s) Olive(s)
agua Water
ajo Garlic
arroz (moro) Rice (with black
  beans)
atún Tuna
azúcar Sugar
bacalao Cod
bacón Bacon
batido Milkshake
bibida Drink

bistec (de puerco) Steak (Pork)
bocadillo / bocadito Sandwich
brocheta Skewer
café Coffee
carne Meat
cebolla Onion
cerdo (asado) Pork (Roast)
cerveza Beer
chatinos Sliced plantain chips
cherna Sea bass
chicharritas Thin, crispy, fried
  plantain slices
chicharrón Fried pork rind

FRUTAS (FRUITS)
fruta bomba Papaya
guayaba Guava
mamey Brown-skinned fruit with orange flesh
melón Watermelon
naranja agria) Orange
piña Pineapple
plátano fruta Banana

chorizo Spicy sausage

chuleta Chop

coco Coconut

camarones Prawns

congrí Rice with red beans

cortado Espresso with a shot
of milk

enchilado/a Stew

ensalada mixta Mixed salad

ensalada de frutas Fruit salad

entremés Hors d'oeuvres
(usually olives and sliced
ham and cheese)

frijoles Beans

frito Fried

garbanzos Chickpeas

guayaba Fruit or coconut jam

harmburgesa Hamburger

helado Ice cream

hielo Ice

huevo(s) Egg(s)

jamón Ham

jugo Juice

langosta Lobster

leche Milk

lechuga Lettuce

limón Lemon

manzana Apple

mariscos Seafood

mermelada Jam

moros y cristianos Black beans
and rice

offerta Set meal

papas Potatoes

papas fritas French fries
or crisps

pan (con mantequilla) Bread
(with butter)

pargo Red snapper

pepino Cucumber

pescado Fish

picadillo Minced beef

picante Spicy

pimienta Pepper

plátano Banana

pollo Chicken

puerco Pork

queso Cheese

res Beef

revuelto Scrambled

ron Rum

ropas vieja Shredded beef
with onions

sal Salt

salchicha Sausage

salsa Sauce

sopa Soup

té Tea

ternera Veal

tortilla Omelette

toronja Grapefruit

tostada Toasted

vegetales Vegetables

zanahoria carrot

DRINKS

Refrescos are fizzy drinks and widely available. It is inadvisable to drink the tap water, and the cautious may refuse to have ice in drinks. Cubans drink lots of strong coffee. Order café espresso for a straight shot, or café con leche if you want milk. Cristal is the most poplar beer, with stronger, 5.4% Bucanero, branded '100% Cubano' a close second. Cuba has started to produce some wines, under the Sorao label, which are light, cheap and sweet and definitely not for the wine connoisseur. Good Spanish, Chilean and some Italian bottles are on the wine list at international resorts.

Of course, Cuba produces excellent, world-renowned rum, made from sugar cane syrup. Order a mojito (rum, lime juice, fresh mint, sugar, and soda water) or a daiquiri (light rum, sugar, lemon juice, and shaved ice). The *cuba libre* ('Free Cuba'), rum and Coke with a squeeze of lime, was created during the Spanish-American war at the beginning of the 20th century and named in a toast by one of the soldiers.

DESSERTS

Cuban *helado* (ice cream) is delicious and there are at least 14 brands available, with Coppelia's ice cream being one of the most famous. *Flan* is baked custard with a caramel glaze served in individual portions. Cubans also make coconut and pumpkin flan of Spanish origin. *Pudin* (bread pudding) is a Spanglish dish that is delicious. *Guayaba* is a kind of jam, usually made from papaya or coconut and often served with cheese.

SNACKS & STALLS

Like all private business in Cuba, street stalls are government regulated, so hygiene is not the problem it can be in other countries. Cuban pizza bought on the street is excellent. Other street foods worth trying are *batidos* (roasted or breaded pork cutlet sandwiches), *pan con tortilla* (bread with egg) and *maní en grano* (peanut brittle). Keep an eye out for

▶ *Pick up a tasty snack at a government-regulated street stall*

stalls and windows with 'comida criolla' signs, where cajitas ('little boxes') are sold. These are meals of salad, baked vegetables and pork cutlets sold in small take-away boxes.

VEGETARIANS

Strict vegetarians who do not eat fish will have a hard time in Cuba, where the diet is traditionally carnivorous. Time of year plays a part too. For example, fruit and vegetables are harder to find in the hottest months (June to September). Vegetarianism might be interpreted as no meat in the soup, where any lumps of meat have been picked out just before serving. However, after a nationwide educational campaign, Cubans have become more aware of the benefits of a vegetarian diet, and new vegetarian restaurants have opened in Havana. Some chefs in restaurants and cooks in casas particulares may already have had experience of cooking meatless dishes, so it is always worth asking what is available or if dishes can be adapted.

⬤ Fresh fruit and vegetables are more widely available in the winter months

Shopping

Cubans have to queue for everything from ice cream to shoes, something to bear in mind if you struggle to find the right gift. The country's current economic situation means that choices of souvenirs are somewhat limited. A t-shirt with a picture of 'Che', bearing one of his famous slogans, some locally grown coffee, and a bottle of rum, all quintessentially Cuban souvenirs, may be as good as it gets.

BUYING CIGARS

The best Cuban cigars are completely hand-rolled and packed in sealed, stamped cedar boxes. There are 42 types and sizes of Havana cigars, classified as fine, medium or thick. Choosing the right cigar requires a degree of knowledge. Examine individual cigars to make sure they are tightly rolled and without any air pockets. The covering should be smooth as silk and all cigars in a box should have a uniform shape, although the colour can vary slightly. Unless you know your cigars well, it is advisable to pay more, to be sure of what you're getting. The five numbered varieties of Montecristo are among Cuba's most popular cigars, and another classic is the stronger Partagás, rolled in Havana since 1845. The milder Romeo y Julieta was invented in 1903.

Cuban cigars are an obvious buy, but beware of fakes. And note that when leaving the country with more than 23 *habanos*, you must show your receipt and the cigar case with its holographic seal. Without the correct documentation, your purchases will be confiscated. English customs regulations allow you to bring 50 cigars into the country.

If you are tempted to buy cigars from a salesperson on the street as a way to save money, think again – nine times out of ten the contents will be fake. To make sure you have the real thing, go to a reputable hotel shop or better still, a cigar factory, and obtain two copies of an official receipt (one to be retained by you and the other to be handed to customs officials on departure).

⬥ *Visit a cigar factory for genuine Cuban cigars*

ART & CERTIFICATION

Any art you buy – and there's a good choice – should in theory at least, be presented at customs on departure with a receipt (in the case of an original piece from an official outlet) or an export certificate (if you have bought a painting or sculpture directly from the artist or a market stall), particularly if the object won't fit inside your suitcase. Getting such a certificate is a lengthy process, which involves taking the artwork to the Registro Nacional de Bienes Culturales (ⓐ Calle 17 No 1009 e/ Calles 10 & 12, Vedado, Havana 🕒 Mon–Fri 09.00–noon) for inspection. You will have to queue for several hours, pay a fee of around $20 or more and return 24 hours later to collect both your art and certificate. Some artists will offer to obtain the permit for you on payment of a deposit. If you don't obtain the certificate, your artwork could be confiscated at the airport.

ANTIQUES

Casas de Comisiones, found in most major towns and cities, are treasure houses full of furniture, lamps and ornaments from Cuban homes, many of which are antiques. Good vintage clothing is also available. All prices are in *moneda nacional*, not Cuban Convertibles. Obviously, for bigger pieces, shipping will need to be arranged, which these shops can usually help with.

DUTY FREE

Cigars, rum, music and anything with Che on it, and more , can be purchased in hotel and souvenir shops, but if you want the best, go to specialist shops, many of which are in Havana. Restrictions apply on the quantity of goods you can bring back in to the UK, duty free. These quantities may change, so check with your travel agent before you leave.
Alcohol One litre over 22% ABV (38% proof), e.g. Whisky Rum, or 2 litres under 22% ABV, e.g. Champagne, Port, Sherry.
Tobacco 200 cigarettes or 50 cigars or 100 Cigarrillos or 250g of tobacco.
Perfumes 50 g (2 fluid ounces) and 250cc eau de toilette.
Allowances are per person, but passengers under 17 are not entitled to tobacco and alcohol.

OPENING TIMES

Generally, shops are open between 09.00 and 17.00 daily except Monday, and usually they close for lunch for an hour from noon or 13.00. Don't expect opening times to be written in stone in the same way as at home.

● *Keep an eye out for unique souvenirs*

Sports & activities

With 5746 km (3570 miles) of coastline, Cuba is great for water sports, particularly deep-sea fishing, and has superb scub diving suitable for all levels. With its mostly flat landscape and practically traffic-free roads, Cuba seems to have been made for cyclists, whether for short trips or longer tours. Fans of walking and horse riding will also find good routes through wonderful countryside.

IN THE WATER

Diving and snorkelling are excellent in Cuba, with a variety of superb sites. There are more than 30 dive centres, managed by either **Marinas Puertosol** (Ⓦ www.puertosol.net), **Cubanacán** (Ⓦ www.cubanacan.cu) or **Cubamar** (Ⓦ www.cubamarviajes.cu). Equipment quality does vary, but you can expect safe, professional diving with these operators. Prices between the sites are comparitively priced. Varadero (see page 39) has over 30 dive sites, but only one with shore access. Other popular areas are Guardalavaca (see page 65), Cayo Coco (see page 55) and Playa Girón on the famous Bay of Pigs.

You don't have to go very deep to enjoy Cuba's warm, tropical waters. Snorkelling provides a multitude of underwater treasures. In Varadero daily snorkelling tours to Cayo Blanco promise abundant tropical fish and good visibility. Cayo Largo (see page 50) offers good boat dives for snorkelling. As in any country, resist the temptation to collect (or buy) coral or shells, and remember to practise responsible diving and snorkelling (for example, avoid touching or standing on the reef).

ON THE WATER

Windsurfing boards, kayaks and jet-skis can be rented from many of the larger resorts. Surfing is possible between November and April, but bring your own board.

Big-game fishing in Cuba was made famous by writer Ernest Hemingway. Particularly big catches of tuna, swordfish, mackerel and sailfish can be had along the north-west coast, where the fast-moving

Gulf Stream supports prime game fishing. Facilities for those who want to try deep-sea fishing for fun are on offer at Varadero (see page 45), Cayo Largo (see page 53) and Playas del Este (see page 32). Fly-fishing is also available at the resorts.

ON THE ROAD

Walking There are kilometres of open road and lovely countryside on offer in Cuba for keen walkers. The most challenging is a three-day hike over the Sierra Maestra mountain range. This and many of the other longer treks require a guide. Check with a travel agency to see what is available in your area. There are some pretty walks around Trinidad, Viñales and Santiago, which are shorter and do not require a guide.

Cycling Decent roads and wonderful scenery, plus the chance to get off the beaten track, make cycling a very popular tourist pastime in Cuba. You can rent a bike from individuals or ask at your resort, as many places have bikes included with your stay or tour.

Horse riding This is a great way to see the countryside and save on the legwork – and it is widely available. Check with your resort.

GO UNDERGROUND

Cuba is riddled with Caves – over 20,000 – and cave exploration is on offer to both tourists and professionals. The Gran Caverna de Santo

◗ *See Cuba from a unique vantage point – on horseback!*

Tomás near the beautiful **Valley of Viñales** (see page 73) is Cuba's largest cavern, with over 46 km (29 miles) to see. Half-day tours from Varadero to **Cuevas de Bellamar** caves near Matanzas (see page 45) have daily tours which include lunch and optional snorkelling.

TAKE YOUR OWN

Taking your own snorkel mask, fins etc is a good idea if you intend to spend much time snorkelling, as the hire gear in Cuba can be often be quite old and tatty. And of course, if you want to donate any of your gear at the end of your trip, it will be gratefully received.

🔺 *Water sports are an option at almost every Cuban beach*

Kids

In Cuba's family-oriented society, children are very much seen and heard and travellers with children will find a friendly welcome in restaurants, theatres and other venues. This means that although Cuba does not have many obvious attractions for children, being on holiday with your offspring here is more likely to be a pleasure than a chore.

WATER SPORTS

There are plenty of activities that will appeal to kids, the most obvious of which are based around the beach. The sun, sand and sea will keep even terrible twos and temperamental teenagers amused for hours. The underwater world provides a temporary distraction – seen from boat tours at Cayo Coco (see page 59) and Varadero (see **Varasub** page 40) and at aquariums in Havana and Guardalavaca (see page 65). At the **Delfinario** near Varadero (see page 41), trained dolphins in captivity perform three times a day, and you can pay extra to swim with them.

HOTEL ACTIVITIES

Various activities are provided by many of the larger hotels in the resorts, many of which are geared towards younger members of the family. At **Cayo Largo**, for example, if you're staying at one of the Sol Meliá or Gran Caribe hotels, you can use the facilities of any of their other hotels (see page 50). This means that your all-inclusive holiday has a little more variety from day to day – kids, in particular, will enjoy trying out the full range of pools and games rooms. Check with your rep or hotel for details.

OTHER KIDS' ACTVITIES

Novelty transport in the form of horse-drawn carriages, cocotaxis, boat trips, rides in vintage cars (page 116), as well as Trinidad's steam train, make travelling fun, and there are 'Noddy Trains' running on both Cayo Coco and Cayo Guillermo. For something different, try the Valle de la Prehistoria at Baconao, where there is a **Dinosaur Trail** (see page 78). Nearby, sharks and sea lions can be seen from a viewing tunnel at the aquarium **Acuario Baconao** (see page 78). **Cayo Iguana** (see pages 52–53), home to a large iguana colony, offers children a great chance to see these fascinating creatures close up. The daily magic shows and scary bats in the cave **Cueva del Jabali** at Cayo Coco (see page 56) will also keep the kids entertained.

STOCK UP BEFORE YOU GO

Items such as baby formula, wipes, disposable nappies, crayons, medicines and sun block simply aren't available in Cuba or are difficult to find, so make sure to pack what you need. Cubans are very resourceful, however, so they will happily whip up vegetable and bean baby food or a cloth nappy.

● Get up close and personal with Cuba's wildlife on Cayo Iguana

Festivals & public holidays

Carnaval, or Carnival, is the highlight of Cuba's festive calendar. It traditionally marked the end of the sugar harvest and was a time when the slaves were allowed to enjoy themselves. Today, Cuban Carnival is a lively outdoor event, fuelled by rum, with colourful processions, traditional bands, sound systems playing international dance music and Muñecones, huge satirical figures of politicians and other famous faces.

The biggest and best of Carnival takes placed in **Santiago de Cuba** at the end of July and at the beginning of August. Havana celebrates in late February and early March, with other smaller festivals held in the capital throughout the year.

There's almost always something on throughout the year in Cuba, particularly in the capital. On 1 January **Liberation & New Year's Day** is celebrated with big street parties countrywide and dozens of outdoor concerts in Havana. For sports fans, the **Baseball Playoffs**, at various locations, feature two weeks of top ball playing during April. During the **Romerías de Mayo** (first week of May) rap, rock, poetry and dance take over Holguín in one of Cuba's most popular events. By contrast, international bolero stars move crowds to tears at the **Festival International Boleros de Oro** in Havana, Santiago de Cuba and elsewhere (third week of June). See Cuba's best contemporary art in mid-November at the **Bienal de la Habana**, a real art extravaganza (next one 2007), and for ballet fans the **Festival International de Ballet** in mid-October – held every two years (next one 2006) – is a tremendous event packed with performances, morning, noon and night.

The most important date in the Cuban revolutionary calendar is 26 July. It is a good time to be in Cuba because it coincides with a number of local carnivals, and if you are lucky you may even see El Commandante, Fidel Castro, speaking in person, although it is likely to be only from a very long distance.

PUBLIC HOLIDAYS

Christmas, suspended in 1969, was only put back on the calendar in anticipation of the Pope's historic visit to Cuba in 1998, during which he spoke out against the US trade embargo.

Cuba has very few public holidays. However, on the days listed below, all banks and most shops are closed.

- **1 January**   Liberation Day
- **1 May**   Labour Day
- **25–27 July**   Celebration of the National Rebellion
- **10 October**   Day of Cuban Culture
- **25 December**   Christmas Day

MORE ABOUT CUBA

- The country's national tree is the **Royal Palm**, and you will see this elegant tree almost everywhere on the island. Resilient and independent, it is seen as symbolic of the Cuban people. The way it is cultivated and used is characteristic of the hatred of waste displayed by the Cuban people, who often say: "We have to look after things because we may not get another". The palm provides wood and other material for rural construction, it is also used to make hats and oils. Parts of it are even used in the tobacco industry.
- The Cuban flag has:
  3 blue stripes for the states into which the island was divided when the flag was first hoisted in 1850;
  2 white stripes representing the idealistic independence fighter;
  1 red triangle standing for the republican ideals of equality, fraternity and liberty, as well as the blood spilled during the fight for independence;
  1 white star, which is the symbol of the freedom of all nations.

⬤ *Public holidays are a time to relax and celebrate*

- The national flower is the **Butterfly Jasmine**, an emblem of insurrection during the wars of independence, which grows wild in humid places as well as being cultivated in homes.
- The Revolutionary Government outlawed racism soon after it came to power and all Cubans are encouraged to think of themselves as mixed-race.
- One in two houses in Cuba has been built since the Revolution.
- One or two children are the norm for the Cuban family, mostly because of economic difficulties.
- Children as young as four can recognize a picture of Che Guevara, a Cuban Revolutionary leader who has been dead for almost 40 years.
- Cuba's national bird is the **Tocororo** – its white, red and blue feathers match the nation's flag.

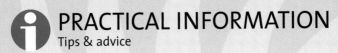

PRACTICAL INFORMATION
Tips & advice

Preparing to go

GETTING THERE

Most tour operators offer a package that includes two or three nights
in Havana, followed by a beach holiday in one of the popular resort
destinations. The flying time from London to Havana is around ten
hours, with international flights from the UK also landing at large
resorts such as Varadero, Cayo Coco, as well as the city of Holguín for
tourists heading to Guardalavaca.

CLIMATE

Cuba is hot year-round, so there isn't really a bad time to go if you are
after sun. However, July and August can be unbearably hot and these
are also the peak holiday months, when hotels are more expensive
and many sights crowded. The hurricane season runs from June to
November, with its peak in September and October. The country has
developed a rapid and efficient response to hurricanes. In October
2005, when Hurricane Wilma slammed into the west coast of Cuba,
700,000 people had already been evacuated, despite the country's lack
of motorized transport.

BEFORE YOU LEAVE

Bring any toiletries, such as insect repellent, sunscreen, tampons,
condoms, contact lens solution and medicine with you, as they can be
hard, if not impossible, to come by in Cuba. Those with digital cameras
probably don't need reminding to bring an adaptor for charging the
battery. A spare battery for times when you are not near a power point
is an even better idea. If you use a traditional camera, stock up on plenty
of film before you leave.

SECURITY

Take sensible precautions while you are away:

- Cancel milk, newspapers and other regular deliveries so that post and
  milk do not pile up on the doorstep.

- Let the postman know where to leave bulky mail that will not go through your letterbox.
- If possible, arrange for a friend or neighbour to visit regularly, closing and opening your curtains, and switching the lights on and off. Or consider buying electrical timing devices that will switch lights and radios on and off.
- Let Neighbourhood Watch representatives know that you will be away so that they can keep an eye on your home.
- If you have a burglar alarm, make sure that it is working properly and is switched on when you leave (you may find that your insurance policy requires this). Ensure that a neighbour is able to gain access to the alarm to turn it off, just in case it is set off accidentally.
- If you are leaving cars unattended, put them in a garage, if possible, and leave a key with a neighbour in case the alarm goes off.

If you are bringing travellers' cheques, bring the receipt you were given when you paid for them in the UK. Many banks and hotels will demand to see this when you change them for Cuban money here.

DOCUMENTS

All visitors to Cuba, regardless of their nationality, must be in possession of a passport valid for six months from date of entry into the country, an onward ticket and a hotel booking for at least the first three nights of their holiday. UK citizens must also have a tourist card, known as a *tarjeta de tourista*, which is issued by your travel agency (or airline if you are buying a flight only). Be sure to check with your travel agent for current prices.

INSURANCE

Do you have sufficient cover for your holiday? Check that your policy covers you adequately for loss of possessions and valuables, for activities you might want to try – such as scuba diving, horse riding, or water sports – and for emergency medical and dental treatment, including flights home if required.

AIRPORT PARKING & ACCOMMODATION

If you intend to leave your car in an airport car park while you are away, or stay the night at an airport hotel before or after your flight, you should book well ahead to take advantage of discounts or cheap, off-airport parking. Airport accommodation gets booked up several weeks in advance, especially during the height of the holiday season. Check whether the hotel offers free parking for the duration of the holiday – often the savings made on parking costs can significantly reduce the accommodation price.

CHECK-IN, PASSPORT CONTROL & CUSTOMS

First-time travellers can often find airport security intimidating, but it is all very easy, really.

- Check-in desks usually open two or three hours before the flight is due to depart. Arrive early for the best choice of seats.
- Look for your flight number on the TV monitors in the check-in area, and find the relevant check-in desk. Your tickets will be checked and your luggage taken. Take your boarding card and go to the departure gate. Here your hand luggage will be X-rayed and your passport checked.
- In the departure area, you can shop and relax, but watch the monitors that tell you when to board – usually about 30 minutes before take-off. Go to the departure gate shown on the monitor and follow the instructions given to you by the airline staff.

BAGGAGE ALLOWANCE

Baggage allowances vary according to the airline, destination and class of travel, but 20 kg (44 lb) per person is the norm for luggage that is carried in the hold (it usually tells you what the weight limit is on your

TELEPHONING CUBA

To call Cuba from the UK, dial 00 53 then the city or area code (see page 120) and the local number.

ticket). You are also usually allowed one item of cabin baggage weighing no more than 5 kg (11 lb), and measuring 46 by 30 by 23 cm (18 by 12 by 9 inches). In addition, you can usually carry your duty-free purchases, umbrella, handbag, coat, camera, etc. as hand baggage. Large items – bicycles, golf-clubs, collapsible wheelchairs and pushchairs – are usually charged as extras and it is a good idea to let the airline know in advance if you want to bring these.

MONEY

Money is a constant issue in Cuba, and not just for locals. In November 2004, the US dollar (which had been introduced as a temporary measure to boost the economy) ceased to be legal currency. If you do bring dollars to change, you will be charged a 20% conversion fee, and even euros attract a 10% change fee.

If you are not planning to leave your resort, you may be able to get by with euros – these are accepted in Varadero, Cayo Coco, Guardalavaca and Cayo Largo. Otherwise, as a tourist you will need to become familiar with the *peso convertible* (CUC), which has almost the same value as the US dollar. As the CUC is a closed currency, it cannot be used or changed outside Cuba and you must change money on arrival and convert any remaining currency on departure.

The dual economy makes things even more complicated – Cubans do not earn CUCs, but Cuban pesos, or *moneda nacional*. Even more confusing is that the $ sign is used to indicate both CUCs and *moneda nacional*. In the main resorts, all prices will be in CUCs, and in main cities the only places operating in *moneda nacional* will be the run-down shops and restaurants that cater to locals.

ATMs There are practically no ATMs dispensing cash for Maestro and Cirrus cards. You may, however, be able to use a Visa or Mastercard at an ATM to withdraw money or to pay in hotels and some restaurants. That is, as long as it has not been issued by an American bank. Check this before you go, because even if your card was supplied in the UK, it may be an American card branded by a UK company – Virgin credit cards are an example of this – and you will not be able to use it anywhere in Cuba.

Travellers' cheques If you bring travellers' cheques make sure they have not been issued by a US company, such as American Express. Thomas Cook travellers' cheques are a good bet, as Cuban resorts are familiar with them.

The money situation in Cuba has undergone several changes in the past few years and many British banks are not up-to-date on the currency situation. Some of the information here may not be current when you travel, so please check with your travel agent before you go.

When you change your travellers' cheques, you may have to show your bank receipt from home, so have it with you. You can change money at hotels and most hotel receptions, but at a poor exchange rate. State-run CADECAS (look for the sign with the $ symbol) offer a better exchange rate both for changing money and cash advances on visa (for which they charge a 3% fee).

If all else fails, contact **Asistur**, which charges a hefty 10% commission to transfer money from either National Westminster or HSBC. The process can take up to five days, but is usually quicker. Asistur has offices throughout Cuba and are generally efficient. Unlike most countries in the world, you cannot receive funds from the UK through Western Union.

ⓐ Prado 208 e/ Colón y Trocadero, Havana (ⓣ (7) 866 4499, ext 127) – the answer machine message in Spanish requests you to enter an extension number. Extension 127 will get you though to an Asistur agent. They also have an office in Varadero (ⓣ (45) 667 277), as well as in Santiago de Cuba, Cienfeugos, Camagüey and Holguín. Check the website (ⓦ www.asistur.cu) for details

---

For some Cubans, even soap is a precious commodity. If you have any spare toiletries, it is a good idea to give them to people who you think might appreciate it. Alternatively, leave them in your hotel room on departure for your maid.

During your stay

ADDRESSES

In Cuba, a street name (*calle, avenida*, etc) is followed by the building number (*numero* or hash symbol). The address is located in relation to one or two cross streets – *esquina* (corner) or *entre* (between). For example: 'Calle Obispo 421, esquina O'Reilly'. In this book, all street names are followed by the number, then if relevant 'e/' for cross or corner, and then the name of the intersecting street.

CRIME & SAFETY

Stiff penalties are in place for any kind of crime against tourists. A young Cuban woman who stole a visitor's wallet was recently sentenced to ten years in prison, and here the full term is always served. As a result, Cuba is, and feels, a very safe destination, even in big cities at night. Take normal precautions, however, and don't carry large amounts of cash with you, flaunt valuables or put yourself in positions where you could be at risk. Be particularly wary of jewellery, wallets and bags while sitting in pavement cafés.

Use a high-factor sun block when out in the sun and reapply it regularly. Take special care when on a boat, as the sea breeze is deceptive and the reflection of the water increases the intensity of the sun. When swimming, take note of warning flags. A red flag indicates that bathing is dangerous and not allowed; yellow means that swimming is permitted, but only with caution; green means it is safe to swim.

ACCESS FOR VISITORS WITH DISABILITIES

Although any kind of discrimination is illegal in Cuba and travellers with disabilities receive much better health care than just about anywhere else in Latin America, access is practically non-existent. Some of the more modern hotels in the large resorts have a limited number of rooms for visitors with disabilities, which should be booked well in advance. The best access is in the more modern resort hotels. The Senador in Cayo Coco even has access to the beach for visitors with disabilities.

ELECTRICITY

You will need an adaptor for electrical goods such as hair dryers, mobile telephones, digital cameras and music players. Electrical outlets are generally 2-pin 110V 50Hz.

 If you are bringing a number of electrical goods, you may want to bring just one voltage adaptor and a four-way UK adaptor. However, don't connect high-current appliances like hair dryers at the same time as charging a camera or phone.

EMBASSIES

In the UK:

Embassy of the Republic of Cuba ⓐ 167 High Holborn, London, WC1V 6PA ⓣ 020 7240 2488

Cuban Consulate ⓐ 15 Grape Street, London WC2 8DR ⓣ 0891 880 820 (recorded message)

In Cuba:

British Embassy ⓐ Calle 34 702/4 e/ 7ma Avenida y 17, Miramar Havana, Cuba ⓣ (7) 204 1771 ⓦ www.britishembassy.gov.uk/cuba

GETTING AROUND

Air Cuba's domestic air service is extensive, reasonably reliable and inexpensive. Internal flights are best booked from the UK as part of a package because prices will probably be cheaper and seats get booked up quickly.

Train A more interesting, if slower and less reliable, option is to take a train. Cuba is the only country in the Caribbean to have a railway and the network has enjoyed good investment over the years, although the vehicles are old. Bear in mind, though, that the train network does not cover the whole country.

Car Hire Cars are in short supply in Cuba, and not just for locals. Even if you have pre-booked a car from home, you might have to wait a day or two to collect it. Extra time will be added onto your contract, so the important thing is not to schedule your trip too tightly. However, do insist on the car you booked, and as a last resort, say you will cancel and try elsewhere. When you get to the office you may be told they only have a bigger car available for more money. Another ruse is to say you can't drop your car off in a different city, which is probably not true.

Even though all car hire offices are government run, rates are, up to a point, negotiable. There should be a discount for hiring a vehicle for a long period. If you feel you are being hustled, ask to see an official, printed price list – they are usually not on display, but are kept hidden away in a drawer somewhere. You can usually pay up-front for the minimum period you think you will need and add on more days later if you want to. Usually, only 24 hour's notice is required for an extension, which is partly why there are never enough cars in the right place. If you have the option, and plan on doing any significant amount of driving, hire a 4x4 (see 'Roads', below).

 If you do want to explore, remember that Cuba is a large island and distances may take longer to cover than you might imagine.

Roads Driving is on the right. The road network is one of the most developed in Latin America, with ring roads allowing you to avoid big cities and a significant stretch of *Autopista* (motorway) running from Pinar del Río in the west to Santiago in the east, albeit with gaps. However, motorways here are not like those at home: few stretches are lit, lane markers are rare, and common sights in the fast lane are children on bicycles, pedestrians, broken-down trucks, and a variety of animals. In addition to this, the potholes on the *Autopista* are often worse than on minor roads that receive less heavy use, so don't expect to get anywhere fast.

Most Cubans do not have cars, and the ones that do drive know the roads, so signposts are not considered a priority. A good road map is essential, but they are not easily available in Cuba, so if possible, get one before you leave. Don't pay any fine direct to the police, as it will be added to the car contract (which you must always have with you when driving) for payment when the vehicle is returned.

Try to pick up hitchhikers whenever you can, as *hacer botella* (literally 'to make a bottle' with the hand) is the only form of transport available to many people. You'll be doing a good deed and your temporary passengers can direct you as you drive. Provided you feel comfortable with the situation, this is a great opportunity to meet and speak with ordinary people.

Taxis By British standards, taxis in Cuba are cheap, but tourists are often taken for a ride. If a taxi has a meter, the fare is non-negotiable, but it may transpire that the meter is broken, so you should always ask before getting into a taxi, and agree a price in the absence of a working meter. Destinations should also be clearly established before setting out.

Taxis that should have meters are the state-run Panataxis, Turistaxis and Habanataxis. The last two are usually modern and comfortable but more expensive, while Panataxis are often Ladas with blue markings but a bit cheaper. Private taxis can usually be hailed on the street, and will not have a licence.

 Taxi drivers are rarely able (or perhaps, willing) to change any note larger than $5 CUC, so try to keep a full supply of smaller notes and coins.

Cocotaxis (Yellow, egg-shaped three-wheeled vehicles) and bicitaxis (cycle rickshaws) in Havana and some other big cities can be fun, especially if you have children. They don't always work out cheaper than standard taxis, and because you are open to the elements, they are best used for shorter journeys in good weather.

If you want to drive around in one of those **vintage American cars** that Havana is famous for, you can hire one with a driver through Gran Car in Havana (☏ (7) 833 5647).

HEALTH CARE

One benefit of state-run television and media is that Cubans are well educated about current health matters. Fruit and salads are integrated into the daily diet, and few Cubans smoke – not just because of the cost, but because they are properly informed about its adverse affects. Castro even gave up smoking his beloved cigars, in public at least, to set a good example to the population, and post Revolution, the life expectancy of Cubans has risen substantially.

Medical care is of a very high standard and there are pharmacies in all the big cities and resort, but because of shortages, it is better to come prepared. Bring any prescription medicines with you, along with a basic first-aid kit. Some visitors come to Cuba for the sole purpose of using the health service here, as highly qualified doctors and nurses can carry out many procedures for a reasonable charge.

THE LANGUAGE

Spanish is the official language, although it is spoken rather differently than in Spain. Even a smile and simple *buenas dias* (hello) can work wonders, and the Cubans are incredibly patient with those who try to speak a few words of their language.

ENGLISH	SPANISH (pronunciation)
General vocabulary	
yes	*si* (see)
no	*no* (no)
please	*por favor* (por faVOR)
thank you (very much)	*(muchas) gracias* (MOOcaahs) GRAseeyas)
you're welcome	*de nada* (de NAda)
hello	*hola* (ola)
goodbye	*adios* (adeeYOS)
good morning/day	*buenas dias* (BWEnas DEEyas)
good afternoon/evening	*buenas tardes* (BWEnas TARdes)

ENGLISH	SPANISH (pronunciation)

General vocabulary cont'd

good evening (after dark)	*bueanas noches* (BWEnas NOches)
excuse me (to get attention)	*disculpe* (desKOOLpay)
excuse me (to apologise)	*perdón* (perDON)
sorry	*lo siento* (lo seeYENtoe)
help!	*socorro!* (SOHcohroe)
today	*hoy* (oy)
tomorrow	*manana* (manYAna)
yesterday	*ayer* (ayYER)
where?	*dónde?* (donday)
when?	*cuándo?* (KWANdo)
why?	*porque?* (porKAY)
how?	*cómo?* (Como)

Useful words & phrases

How much is it?	*Cuánto es?* (KWANtoe es)
Expensive	*Caro/a* (KARo/a)
I don't understand	*No entiendo* (no enteeYENdoe)
Do you speak English?	*Hablar usted Ingles?* (ablah OOsted eenGLES)
My name is...	*Me llamo...* (meh YAmoh..)

MEDIA

Granma is the official Cuban Communist Party paper, and is published in English and Spanish. No British newspapers are on sale, and there is a limited selection of American and European magazines. There may be an Internet service at your hotel, which you can access with a pre-paid card and password, but don't expect connections to be as fast as at home.

There are two national television stations: Cubavision and Tele Rebelde. The first shows soap operas and films; the second, features news, sports and talk shows. Most large hotels have the English-language channels Cinemax, HBO and CNN, as well as the Spanish-language ESPN Deportes, which sometimes shows Premiership football.

OPENING HOURS

Banks These close at noon on the last working day of the month, but otherwise are open 09.00–15.00.

Exchange offices Open Mon–Sat 09.00–18.00; Sun 09.00–noon

Chemists Those marked with a sign saying *turno permanente* or *pilotos* are open 24 hours. Others open 08.00–20.00.

Post offices Main post offices stay open later than the smaller ones, which are open Mon–Sat 08.00–18.00.

Shops Opening times vary, but all are generally closed on Sunday afternoons.

PHOTOGRAPHY

Cubans are incredibly photogenic, but do always ask first before taking a photograph. You may be asked for a tip, but if you hand over money it only encourages begging. Instead, ask the person for their address so you can send them a print. This gesture will be much appreciated, as photographs are too expensive for most Cubans. Good film is expensive and developing is of a poor quality and expensive, so it's best to bring your own film if you are not using digital.

POST

Many larger hotels sell stamps (*sellos*) for postcards and will even post them for you, which is much easier than going to a post office. Delivery can be slow: around three weeks is the norm, but expect to wait anything up to two months. Pre-paid postcards, including international postage, are available at most hotel shops and post offices and are the best bet for successful delivery. For important mail, you are better off using DHL, located in all the major cities.

TELEPHONE

Like everywhere else in the world, calls from hotel rooms are very expensive. However, unlike most other countries, international calls with difficult-to-use prepaid phone cards (purchased from hotels and local shops) work out just a fraction cheaper than hotel rates. Dial 012 for an

English-speaking international operator if you want to make a reverse charge call.

At the time of writing, Cuba has two mobile phone companies: c.com and Cubacel (Ⓦ www. cubacel.com). While you may be able to use your own equipment, you have to prebuy their services. Cubacel has over 15 offices around the country, inluding one at Havana airport, where you can do this. If you have a modern handset, the chances are it will work in Cuba (check with your provider before leaving the country), but the costs can be astronomical – not just to make calls, but to receive them (as anyone calling from the UK is charged at the normal rate to an British mobile and you are charged the rest). If you do need to bring your phone, it is a good idea to limit it to text messages only, which are likely to be much less (but again, check with your provider).

The Cuban phone system has been undergoing extensive reorganization, so check any number if you are having problems. Many city codes have changed, but not all. The eventual aim is to have a single code for each province, although currently the dialling code for some areas of a province might differ from that of the main city. If your Spanish is up to it, directory enquires, on 113, is free.

USEFUL NUMBERS
To call the UK ☎ 119 + area code (minus the 0) + number
Police ☎ 106
Fire department ☎ 105
National directory assistance ☎ 113

TIME
Cuba is five hours behind GMT. From April to September, Cuba is on daylight saving time, during which Cuba is only four hours behind GMT.

However, 'Cuban Time' is a phenomenon you may not be familiar with! Expect long queues for everything from changing money to hotel check-in. Remember, too, that this is the Caribbean, and during your holiday you will benefit enormously from the laid-back attitude here. Few people will hurry you, mistakes with language, etiquette and culture will go uncorrected, and most people will help you at the drop of a hat.

Not only is the concept of time much more flexible in Cuba, but whether an establishment – including a national museum – stays open or not may depend on how many customers there are. Always have 'Plan B' at the ready.

TIPPING

Musicians who beseige you while you dine, toilet attendants, parking attendants, taxi drivers and tour guides, are all working for hard currency tips. Waiters in upmarket restaurants receive tips on a daily basis, but others receive very little or nothing at all and are reliant on tourists' generosity. As a rough guideline, give a porter, waiter or tour guide $1 CUC, and a maid $3–5 CUC for every week.

Due to the severe shortages in the country, unwanted clothing, pens, paper, and children's toys and games are very welcome. Show consideration when handing these out, however. Cubans, like most people, find it hard to accept handouts. Also, giving goods out in the street only encourages begging. If you do take goods that you want to distribute, try to find a school (preferably away from an obvious tourist area) and give the teacher your bag or 100 biros, for example, for distribution.

TOILETS

Public toilets are practically non-existent in Cuba, although you will find them in bus stations, restaurants and tourist hotels. Unlike at home, you can use the facilities of pretty much any bar or restaurant if you ask in advance. Toilet paper is regarded as a luxury and is not usually provided in the cubicle. Instead, a toilet attendant (sometimes absent, even if the paper and a saucer for tips, isn't) provides paper in exchange for a small coin or two. It is a good idea to carry your own supply. Cuban sewer systems are not designed to take toilet paper or tampons and, aside from top-end hotels and resorts, a small wastepaper basket next to the toilet is provided for this purpose.

TOURIST INFORMATION

In the UK   Cuba Tourist Office (🄰 167 High Holborn, London, WC1V 6PA 🄣 020 7240 6655). The information you will get here is limited. It's a case of leaving your details (if you can get through) and then waiting to see if you will be sent some promotional brochures. Individual queries are rarely dealt with and you may well get more useful information from a half-decent travel agent, or from the Internet. A good idea is to first try the official Cuban tourism websites (🅦 www.cubaweb.cu) and (🅦 www.cubatravel.com).

In Cuba   There is no tourist information service in Cuba. A couple of companies bill themselves as tourist information offices, but are in reality travel agencies. They often sell useful maps, can provide you with leaflets detailing restaurants, bars, hotels and so on. Of course, their main business is to sell you excursions and tours.

You will probably come across **Infotur** in Havana (🄰 Calle Obispo 358 e/ Habana 🄣 Open 09.00–18.00), which also has an office in Santiago de Cuba.

For information in Varadero, consult **Havanatur** 🄰 Ave. Playa 3606 e/ Calle 36 🄣 (045) 63713)

If the lack of tourist information gets to you, try asking a local. Approach a friendly waiter or hotel worker, and avoid *jiniteros* (street hustlers).

WEBSITES

Cuba is not as developed as many other holiday destinations when it comes to the Internet, and there are only a handful of websites providing information about the country; even these are often out of date.

Obviously things are changing, so you may find some of these no longer exist or that new and better sites have replaced them. All of the sites listed below have English pages, usually accessed by clicking the Union Jack or the 'English' button on the main page.

www.Cubanacan.cu This website is operated by Cubanacán, a state-run tourism company that make reservations for hotels, transportation, and excursions. If you email, you are unlikely to get a reply! Cubanacán desks can be found in most hotels.

www.cubasi.cu This basic site is not bad for general news as well as details of cultural events, and its tourism pages provide a different slant on attractions.

www.cubanculture.com A general site with solid information and lots of pictures and a long list of regional pages covering everything from museums to flora.

www.cuba-junky.com A human and thorough approach to the country, although the bright colours and clunky language can be annoying. Fun and informative, it was set up to benefit Cubans and is a not-for-profit website.

www.casaparticular.com One of the few sites with information on both *casas particulares* (private homes where you can stay in Cuban cities) and *paladares* (family-run restaurants).

www.pamarillas.cu This 'yellow pages' site is unfortunately in Spanish only. Operated by the state-run telephone company ETCESA, it can, however, be a useful resource.

www.tripadvisor.com A good source of information about Cuban resorts, hotels and restaurants. Try to consult this site before you book your holiday.

WEIGHTS & MEASURES

Cuba uses the metric system, so the official units of weights and measures are the kilo and the gram. These days most of us are familiar with this, so there should not be much to worry about. Petrol is sold by the litre, not the gallon.

Imperial to metric
1 inch = 2.54 centimetres
1 foot = 30 centimetres
1 mile = 1.6 kilometres
1 ounce = 28 grams
1 pound = 454 grams
1 pint = 0.6 litres
1 gallon = 4.6 litres

Metric to imperial
1 centimetre = 0.4 inches
1 metre = 3 feet, 3 inches
1 kilometre = 0.6 miles
1 gram = 0.04 ounces
1 kilogram = 2.2 pounds
1 litre = 1.8 pints

 INDEX

INDEX

ACKNOWLEDGEMENTS

We would like to thank all the photographers, picture libraries and organisations for the loan of the photographs reproduced in this book, to whom copyright in the photograph belongs:
David Bishop/FoodPix/Getty Images (page 86);
Jeremy Horner/Corbis (page 91);
Jupiter Images Corporation (pages 102, 107, 125);
Marina Spironetti/Alamy (page 92);
Copyright Thomas Cook (page 100);
All other images courtesy of Jane Egginton.

We would also like to thank the following for their contribution to this series:
John Woodcock (map and symbols artwork);
Katie Greenwood (picture research);
Patricia Baker, Rachel Carter, Judith Chamberlain-Webber, Nicky Falkof, Nicky Gyopari, Robin Pridy (editorial support);
Christine Engert, Suzie Johanson, Richard Lloyd, Richard Peters, Alistair Plumb, Jane Prior, Barbara Theisen, Ginny Zeal, Barbara Zuñiga (design support).

Send your thoughts to
books@thomascook.com

- **Found a beach bar, peaceful stretch of sand or must-see sight that we don't feature?**

- **Like to tip us off about any information that needs a little updating?**

- **Want to tell us what you love about this handy, little guidebook and more importantly how we can make it even handier?**

Then here's your chance to tell all! Send us ideas, discoveries and recommendations today and then look out for your valuable input in the next edition of this title. And, as an extra 'thank you' from Thomas Cook Publishing, you'll be automatically entered into our exciting monthly prize draw.

Send an email to the above address or write to:
HotSpots Project Editor, Thomas Cook Publishing, PO Box 227, Unit 15/16, Coningsby Road, Peterborough PE3 8SB, UK.